INTRODUCTION
TO
INFORMATION TECHNOLOGY

INTRODUCTION TO INFORMATION TECHNOLOGY

Editor

Arun Baveja

KALPAZ

ISBN : 978-81-7835-000-4

Published, 2018

Published by

Kalpaz Publications
C-30, Satyawati Nagar,
Delhi – 110052
E-mail: kalpaz@hotmail.com
Website: kalpazpublications.com
Ph.: 011-47034999, 9212142040

Printed at: G. Print Process, Delhi.

Contents

1

Introduction

While mankind has developed a myriad ways of applying and controlling power to dominate and shape our environment, through the use of tools, weapons, machines, fuels, vehicles, instruments, clothing, buildings and roads, metals, plastics and drugs, agriculture, and electricity, the handling of information has lagged considerably, perhaps because the human brain is itself so remarkably powerful.

Until recently, there have been only three major developments in this area: the invention of written (or painted or carved) language, some five or six thousand years ago; that of simple arithmetic operations, using what would now be called a digital representation of numbers, about a thousand years later; and that of printing, about five hundred years ago. With written language, we get the capacity to make a permanent record of information and also to convey messages across space and time: storage, *retrieval*, and *communication*.

With digital arithmetic, we get the ability to perform accurate, repeatable *manipulations* of *quantitative data*. With printing, we can make many identical copies of the same record and so *broadcast* a single message to a wide and continuing audience.

Beyond these outstanding advances, until the last hundred years or so, the only progress has been in the engineering and increasingly plentiful production of more powerful and reliable and efficient, faster and cheaper devices to implement these concepts. In the last hundred years, we see the rapidly accelerating advent of a technology so powerful, novel, widespread, and influential that we may indeed call it the Second Industrial Revolution. Its basis is electromagnetic, in many interconnected forms: photography, photocopying, cinematography, and holography; telegraphy, telephony, radio communication, radar, sonar, and telemetry; sound and video recording and reproduction; vacuum tubes, transistors, printed circuits, masers, lasers, fiber optics, and (in rapid succession) integrated circuits (IC), large-scale integration (LSI), and very large-scale integration (VLSI) of circuitry on a tiny semi-conducting 'chip'; and, finally, the bewildering variety of electronic digital computers.

The progress has been truly amazing. In only about 40 years, electronic communications and news media have become commonplace and indispensable; computers have proliferated, becoming increasingly fast, powerful, small, and cheap, so that now there is scarcely a human activity in which they are not to be found, bearing an increasing share of the burden of repetitive information processing, just as the machines of the First Industrial Revolution have taken over the majority of heavy and unpleasant physical labor. Now, information can not only be stored, retrieved, communicated, and broadcast in enormous quantities and at phenomenal speeds; but it can also be rearranged, selected, marshalled, and transformed.

Until recently, these activities were the sole province of the human brain. While creative, judicious, moral, and esthetic choices are still best left to people, all the tedious and mechanical mental processes can now be relegated to the accurate, fast, and tireless machines. Any sequence of operations on information that can be precisely specified can be carried out without further human intervention or supervision.

At first, computers were the experimental toys of university researchers; then they became the tools of government establishments and giant corporations, huge, expensive, individually designed and manufactured, and beyond the reach of any but the wealthiest organizations.

People thought of the future in terms of machines of ever-greater speed and capacity; centralized behemoths would hold all the world's information in gigantic data banks, whence major decisions would issue to be imposed upon the populations at their mercy.

With the emergence of powerful, cheap, mass-produced computers-on-a-chip, the picture has changed radically. Now we see tiny computers everywhere: in wrist-watches, microwave ovens, electronic games, pocket calculators, cameras, typewriters, musical instruments, etc.

What used to be done, with few options, by intricate mechanical devices is now performed, with great flexibility and convenience and at much less expense, by the ubiquitous preprogrammed microcomputer.

The probable future has become one of millions of small yet powerful computers, controlling virtually every machine and appliance, distributed in every home, on every desk, in every workshop; many of them connected In a maze of small and large networks, much like the present telephone network, so that individual computers could communicate, sharing information in a gigantic distributed data-base, and gaining, through distributed processing, computational power whose extent is yet difficult to gauge; all this following the individual requirements and choices of the owner or operator of each machine. Increasingly, we are confronted, not only with the results of the use of computers throughout industry, commerce, banking, advertising, science, the communications industry, newspapers, airlines, and hospitals; but with the realistic possibility of purchasing computer power for our own small enterprises, offices, and homes. This may be done in a variety of ways; but in all of them, the real cost of computation is constantly diminishing.

It is probably fair to say that the question of computerization is not "whether," but "when" and "how." We must choose whether to lease equipment or to buy it; whether to install terminals, connected to a computerized "service bureau," or a complete local computer system; whether to get a package of standard programs directed towards our kind of work, to commission new programs tailored to our special needs, or to learn programming and write our own; whether to go it alone or to share a system with a number of similar users (especially if they are in the same building); how far to take our first efforts at computerization; what to include and what to continue doing by hand. Computer programming is likely to become the literacy of the third millennium AD.

Elementary schools may well be teaching it before long, and we might be well advised to gain at least a smattering of knowledge of computers and of programming competence, especially since computer languages and programming environments are becoming increasingly helpful and friendly to the uninitiated user.

A computer is a machine for the automatic processing of information. Historically, this information was numerical, and computers were machines for doing arithmetic.

Unlike the simpler calculating machines, which can perform only one elementary arithmetic operation at a time, then need to be told what to do next (usually, by suitable button-pushes); computers can be given a list of operations to perform (often with branching and repetitions, depending on tests of sign or value included among the operations), and will then execute these in proper sequence without further intervention. This sequence of instructions is called a program.

A digital computer stores its information in the form of words, finite ordered sets of digits, each of which can have only one of a finite set of values.

Considerations of simplicity, reliability, and economy dictate that electrical engineers should design computers to consist of a great number of similar pieces of circuitry, each of which can only be in one of two states, usually denoted by 0 and 1.

Such *binary digits* (or bits) are the elements of which computer digital representation is built. A row of eight bits is called a *byte,* and the majority of computers have their storage of information organized in words of one, two, four, or eight bytes (8, 16, 32, or 64 bits).

The number of bits in a word is termed its *length;* if this is *k,* then the number of possible distinct pieces of information that can be stored in such a word is 2 ~ In particular, four bits together can have 16 different contents, and these are standard binary representations of the numbers 0-15:

0000 = 0 0001 = 1 0010 = 2 0011 = 3

0100 = 4 0101 = 5 0110 = 6 0111 = 7

1000 = 8 1001 = 9 1010 = A 1011 = B

1100 = C 1101 = D 1110 E 1111 = F

with A = 10, B = 11, C = 12, D 13, E 14, and F = 15. These may now be viewed as the 16 possible digits of a representation (the hexadecimal, or hex), which is much more compact and humanly intelligible than a long string of zeros and ones. For example, the byte 10110010 becomes "132," and the four-byte computer word

01001100011100101101000110001110 becomes the eight-digit hex word "4C72D18E."

The following are various parts of which any computer is composed. These are, essentially,

1. a *central processing unit* (CPU), which is the controlling and computing centre of the machine;
2. a *memory,* possibly of different levels, in which both *data* and *instructions* are stored;
3. a variety of *input* and *output (I/O) devices,* through which the machine communicates with the world outside it.

The CPU consists of an operation control unit (OCU), an *arithmetic/logical unit* (ALU), and a relatively small, very-fast accessible local memory (LM). The ocu keeps track of the memory location of the next instruction to be executed, and analyzes the current instruction, so as to activate the proper operation of a memory transfer, non-sequential jump (by appropriately changing the address of the next instruction), input or output of information, or computation (performed by the ALU), as is indicated by the instruction code.

The ALU actually carries out the elementary arithmetic operations (addition, subtraction or negation, multiplication, division or reciprocation) and logical operations (these being bit-by-bit operations, without carry' such as not, and, and xor; eg., not 1010= 0010, 1100 and 0101 =0100, 0110 xor 1010 = 1100) on the data given to it by the ocu. The Lm receives the operands called for by the ocu and also the results of the ALU'S operations upon them. For example, the ocu may retrieve the factors of a multiplication from the main memory into a pair Of Lm registers and instruct the ALU to multiply them and place their product in another Lm register. Such registers are usually called accumulators, and they are normally double-length (since the product of two k-bit numbers is a 2k-bit number). Other Lm registers are used for counting (eg. repetitions) and are called index registers; others hold intermediate values and are called buffers; and, finally, there are one-bit or two-bit registers which reflect the information on which tests are made by the ocu (for example, the occurrence of a carry, the vanishing or positivity of an answer, or the occurrence of an arithmetic overflow): these are termed flags.

Originally, the CPU was a sizable piece of electronics, hand-assembled and highly complex. With the advent of micro-miniaturization of circuitry, printing, and photographic techniques, and the mass production of components only the largest computers (mainframes) are built in the old way. Smaller systems generally have the entire CPU on a single chip. Among these, the name microcomputer is now applied to those with less than a million words of memory and a word length of one or two bytes; the name minicomputer applies to the larger machines, with two- to four-byte words and one to a hundred million words of memory. (The smallest micro is probably more powerful than the big computers used by universities and industry in the 1950s.)

The *main memory* (mm) consists of magnetic or electronic components which store the information (both data and instructions) needed by the computer. The individual words are directly addressable from the CPU by number (rather like houses in a street), and their contents are retrievable in very short times, of the order of the operation time of the CPU (ranging from fractions of a *nanosecond*, 10^{-9} or one billionth of a second, for the fastest main-frames to several *microseconds*, 10^{-6} or millionths of a second, for the slower micros). This is often referred to as high-speed storage or random-access memory (RAM). While most of the mm is erasable and may be changed at will, some memory is used to store constants and often-used utility programs and is not erasable by the cpu: such memory is called *read-only memory* (ROM). Sometimes this is optional and can be plugged into the computer: this is called *firmware.*

Note that a computer with one-byte-long addresses can have at most 28= 256 words of mm; a two-byte address can reach 256^2 = 65536 words; a three-byte address can select any of 16777216 words of mm; and so on. In practice, most micros and minis have mm ranging in size from 2 14= 16384 to 218= 262144 words. It should be noted that 10^3= 1000 and 2^{10}= 1024. Because computers are so heavily slanted towards base-2 representation, it has become almost universal computer parlance to use the prefix *kilo* or K (which usually denotes a thousand units) to denote 1024 and the prefix *mega* or M (which usually denotes a million units) to denote 2^{20} = 1024^2 = 1048576. Thus, we write 16K for 2^{14} and ¼M for 2^{18}. Perhaps the commonest size of MM consists of 64K = 65536 words.

Almost all computer instructions comprise an operation code (usually one byte long, allowing 256 possible operations to be specified), followed by an operand reference (number, index, or address) of variable length (since some operations require more data than others; for instance, the STOP instruction needs no operand, so it is one byte long).

The *extended memory* (EM) is sometimes considered under I/O devices, both because it is often physically located outside the computer (while the CPU and the mm are usually in the same enclosure), and because its speed of access is much slower than the speed of operation of the CPU and is comparable with the range of speeds of i/o devices. Most read/write memory is magnetic (optical memory is read-only, and fast RAM is either magnetic or electronic), either in the form of tape, drum, or disk, coated with magnetic material, much like sound-recording equipment; it is similarly erased, read, and recorded upon by "heads" which contain electromagnetic sensors/ polarizers. The cheapest (and most limited, in both speed and capacity) device is a common portable cassette recorder, with 1/4" tape cassettes. From this, one moves to specially engineered cassettes and recorders, and thence to high-speed 1/2" or I" reel-to-reel drives carrying thousands of feet of tape at very high speeds. Access times can be quite good for sequential access, along the tape, but random access time is poor at best, running to seconds or even minutes. Economy and a virtually unlimited total storage capacity (on numerous cassettes or reels; but only as many units as one has on-line tape-drives are actually accessible without human intervention) are the only advantages.

When we wish for practically useful EM, combining large capacity with relative economy and speed of random access, we must turn to drum or disk memory; and, nowadays, the former have been practically replaced by the latter. Disk memory is of two types: floppy disk and hard disk, the first being the cheaper, slower, smaller-capacity option. Floppy disks are flexible, have diameters of 51/4" or 8", generally, and are removable from the disk-drive, so allowing one to build up an unlimited library of stored data. The information is stored on concentric circular tracks (not on a single spiral track, as on a sound record), on one or both sides of the disk. The number of tracks and the number of bytes per track vary (the density increasing with precision of engineering, and so with cost of the drive), but the total capacity of a floppy disk is in the range of 50KB to 1MB. The disks rotate at, typically, 300 rpm, and access time is governed by the time required to place the movable head on the right track, a fraction of a second, plus the fifth of a second taken by the head to traverse the circumference of the track, in search of a record; thereafter, consecutive bytes are accessed at some thousands per second.

Hard disks are rigid and have larger diameters. There are drives with anything from one to a dozen disks, rotating at about ten times the speed of floppy-disk drives (and so diminishing the access time of records in a track) with one or several heads.

Fixed-head drives naturally must have a head for each track (which costs more), but save head-movement time in random access. *Winchester* disks are movable-head drives with sealed-in disks, which the heads ride very close to the disk, cushioned by the layer of air between. In floppy-disk drives, the head actually rides on the disk, eventually wearing it out.

The capacity of hard-disk drive ranges from 10 MB to 100 MB in a single drive. Some movable-head hard-disk drives have removable disks or disk-packs, allowing for greater library storage.

The *I/O devices* are the computer's link with the outside world. In large mainframe computers, we see *paper card* (as in Hollerith or "IBM" cards) and paper tape readers and punches: the perforations in the paper carry the information. Increasingly in large computers, and almost universally in small ones, the main input is from the keyboard of a terminal. This is much like a typewriter keyboard, and depressing any key sends an 8-bit code to the computer.

When the computer is waiting for input from this terminal, it reads the code and interprets it as a datum; when it is busy, either the message is lost or it is held in a "buffer" for subsequent input (this depends on how the connection is made and what the computer is made to do). It is quite common for the computer to be connected to several terminals, all competing for its attention. This is called time-sharing. The computer cycles around the terminals, looking for their several inputs and dividing its CPU time among them. The main output of the computer is to the display devices of the terminals; these are either video displays (cathode ray tubes, CRT, just like the screens of black-and-white or color TV sets; indeed, simple micros sometimes use ordinary television sets as display devices) or printers (in so-called hard-copy terminals). Of course, the computer may be connected to additional video displays and printers, of different qualities, as well as to plotters, a kind of printer for drawing graphs and diagrams. Many types and speeds of printers exist. Other input devices, such as audio amplifiers (receiving signals from radio tuners, record players, etc), video receivers and recorders, laser disk drives and a variety of scientific instruments, can all be classified as transducers (devices that transform physical quantities, such as position, conductivity, pressure, temperature, vibration frequency, or amplitude, into electromagnetic impulses) linked to digitizers (which convert such impulses into sequences of zero/one pulses). Output from the computer can similarly follow the reverse process, yielding visible or audible results, or the control of mechanical or electrical equipment. Thus computers can draw pictures (often, moving pictures), make music and other sounds, and can control appliances, machinery, and whole manufacturing processes.

In order to connect remote terminals to a computer, use is often made of telephone lines; and, for this purpose one employs a device called a modem (for "Modulator/ DEModulator"), which converts the computer's digital signals to and from telephone audio signals. This has a cradle shaped to hold the ear and mouth pieces of a telephone's hand-set. It is also possible to connect several computers in this way. This is called the formation of a computer network. Of course, computers may also be connected by cable, fibre-optics, or microwave link. It should be noted that terminals usually, and other I/O devices often, themselves contain computers of varying degrees of power and complexity; so that even a multi-user computer with a central CPU may stiff be seen as a kind of computer network in its own right. The computers in I/O devices such as terminals or printers are often referred to as peripheral processors (PP).

Many networks do not have a central computer at all; but are simply a collection of independent computers linked for the sharing of information and, sometimes, computing capabilities. Often, they permit the exchange of messages (*computer mail*) and the pooling of data (*distributed data-base*). They may also share a common bank of memory, accessible to all.

Finally, since the invention of computer networks, designers have been investigating the possibilities of computers made up of an array of CPUs (*multicomputers, parallel processors, distributed processing*). These new ideas are very powerful and far-reaching: they will probably revolutionize our ideas of computers, and of their applications, in the next few years.

The various peripheral devices are connected to the CPU without examining how. In fact, this may be done in several ways. We can simply have a separate connection (or port) for each device, but this limits rather severely the number of devices that may be connected to the cpu. Another way Is to have a single bus (or connection) to which any number of devices may be attached.

The information signal must then carry an appropriate address. The bus receives all signals, and individual devices (including the cpu) seek out and decode only those addressed to them. It is also possible to have a switching device, which receives addressed data and directs them to the appropriate recipient device, rather like a central post office.

The decision on what communication arrangements to adopt is made on the basis of considerations of cost, capacity, and speed. It is often the case that the several devices forming a computer or a computer network have their data coded in different ways.

It is then the job of the CPU(s) and PPs to share the work of interpreting signals into appropriate codes for each machine. This is broadly termed the problem of interfacing devices. Sometimes, the solution is to have a standard code or structure for the communications device (one meets the s-100 bus, the rs-232 serial port, the ASCII character-code, and so on).

Another interfacing problem arises from the difference in the rate at which different devices can send and receive information (this is measured by the baud rate, named after Baudot, the inventor of the first five-hole paper-tape code; one baud is one bit transferred per second; hence kilobaud, kb, and megabaud, Mb typical rates range from 200 baud to 200 kb). One solution is to send each piece of information (usually one character at a time, which takes 8 to 10 bits) only when the last has been acknowledged (this is referred to as a handshake); this is sure, but slow. Another way is to use a storage buffer in which a large batch of information is accumulated for fast transmission, thus not wasting the time of the faster device.

One last kind of choice must be mentioned: some channels of communication are serial (they transmit one bit at a time), while others are parallel (they can transmit a byte or a whole word at a time); the latter are obviously faster, more complex, and more expensive. When devices are connected by cable, the degree of parallel communication is exhibited in the width of a flat ribbon cable, carrying several wires, side by side, and in the number of pins in the plugs and sockets by which they are connected to the machines. Parallel transmission is a variation on multiplexing. What we have described is generally referred to as the hardware of a computer. By contrast, the programs that make the computer work, the "soul" of the machine, as opposed to the hardware "body," are collectively called its software. Inevitably, there came to be programs that were hard-wired (in the now outdated phrase) into the computer, in the form of ROM. These are termed firmware.

A computer without software is a helpless set-of circuits, and the expertise required to create the basic software that will bring the machine to useful life is comparable to that required to design the machine itself Indeed, these days, computers are designed in cooperation between computer architects, who design what the computer will do, hardware engineers, who design how it will be constructed to be able to do it, and software engineers, who design and program the operating system that will run the machine. Beyond this, the computer will also need application software of many kinds, to enable it to do a variety of jobs, such as file-handling, accounting, statistics, payrolls, inventories, complex graphic displays, games, and so on.

Typically, the application software is written (i.e. programmed) by the endusers (if they are sophisticated enough) or firms of consultants and programmers and system analysts, often called software houses. Sometimes, a software house will produce part or all of an alternative operating system, or an addition to an operating system, to make a computer more flexible or more efficient than the manufacturer's own software system allows it to be.

COMPUTER LANGUAGES

The CPU of any computer is designed to accept and execute a specific set of *operation codes* (*op-codes*), ranging in number from a dozen or so to several hundred. Different makes and models of computers and microprocessors may have entirely dissimilar op-codes; but the operations that they represent are much more alike than different, both through functional necessity and historical development.

The interpretation of the op-codes is built into the hardware of the ocu (though sometimes the details of interpretation may be modified by the user through what is called *microcoding*), and it is part of this interpretation that the complete instruction being decoded contains a certain amount of further information (such as parameters, indices, and one or more memory addresses).

The "length" of a computer instruction (the number of consecutive memory words, or of bytes, occupied by it) may vary, but the ocu automatically adjusts to this. An executable program (sometimes called "object code") consists of a sequence of machine instructions, consecutively stored in the computer's memory and (with the exception of "jump" instructions) executed in the order in which they are stored.

The aggregate of possible machine instructions is called the machine language. In the computer, a program consists of a long string of binary digits (bits), usually written as 0's and 1's; and, of course, the same program would be interpreted quite differently (usually as nonsense) by any computer for which it is not designed. Indeed, the slightest error in a program almost always leads to an error in its output (usually a fatal error!). This state of affairs is sometimes expressed by the computer adage, "Garbage in; garbage out," or just "GIGO." Errors in programs are called bugs; and the tedious, odious process of finding and correcting such errors is termed debugging. It is estimated that, in the production of a working program, the debugging time may be two to four times as long as the time it takes to plan and write the program initially.

To give the reader a feeling for the nature of machine language, we present a simplified, fictitious, but typical, machine language specification. Our computer has two 16-bit accumulator registers (acc), X and Y, which may be coupled into a single 32-bit ace XY, with X holding the more and Y the less significant digits; these are attached to the ALU; and a program control register (pc) Z, also of 16 bits, attached to the ocu, which contains the address of the next instruction to be executed. Instructions will contain a 2-bit acc code a, with a = 0 referring to X, a = 1 to Y, a = 2 to XY, and a = 3 to Z. The memory consists of 216 = 65536 16-bit words, directly addressable with a 16-bit address, n.

There are four addressing modes, denoted by a 2-bit mode code d, with d=O referring to absolute address (address *n*\0 refers to the actual number "*n*"), *d* = I to direct address (address *n*\1 refers to word n in the memory), *d* = 2 to indirect address (*n*\2 refers to the memory address which is the content of the memory word with address *n*), and *d* = 3 to relative address (*n*\3 refers to the memory address that is the sum of *n* and the content of the pc register Z, with any carry to the seventeenth bit ignored). We will write {{*a*}} for the acc denoted by a, {*n**d*) for the memory word with address *n* in mode *d*, and C[*x*] for the content of word or acc *x* (so, e.g., C[{*n*]2}]=C[C[n]], while C[{*n*\3}]=C[*n*+C[Z]). *A port code p* selects one of 8 *output ports* (*p*=0, 1, . . ., 7) and 8 *input ports* (*p* = 8, 9, . . . , 15), these ports transmitting 16 bits at once and having to be reactivated before each function (i.e., each output instruction sends out one 16-bit number, and the machine must wait for the output to be acknowledged before making another output; while each input instruction reads one 16-bit number, if an input is available, and the machine must wait for a new input each time). Finally, a bit code b refers to each of the 16 bits in a word (bit 0 being the least significant-rightmost-and bit 15 the most significant-leftmost). In some cases, the codes a, d, p, and b are interpreted somewhat differently, depending on the particular op-code c.

As an example of a very simple computer program, we consider the solution to the following computer problem. Our computer is to be fed a sequence of one thousand 16-bit numbers at input port #9 (these may be keyed in by hand or fed in by a digitizer connected to some experiment). They are to be stored in memory words with addresses 5000, 5001, 5002, . . . , 5999. Their sum is to be computed and stored in address 6000 and output to a printer through output port #2. The program is to be stored beginning at address 0 in the memory.

Again, what is important about this example is not its detailed form, but the difficulty of its interpretation, and therefore also the difficulty of verification and debugging.

The programmer must deal with a mass of details that are of a purely mechanical nature and have no relevance to the problem being solved. "Higher-level languages" are attempts at making the computer understand the programmer's way of thinking, rather than forcing the programmer to think like a machine.

HIGHER-LEVEL LANGUAGES

After some introductory description of an imaginary computer, and especially of its CPU, and the establishment of some essential notation. Presented with a set of arithmetic and other transformations required by potential users of a proposed new computer, the electronic and logical design engineers seek the simplest circuitry that will execute operations sufficient to generate all the required transformations. Circuits must be simple to be fast, efficient, reliable, and cheap. However, when an instruction has 16 or more bits, most of which should for the sake of efficiency, have some significant effect; the exact and complete specification of the action induced by it may well be somewhat forbiddingly intricate! And indeed, simplicity of circuitry does not usually lead to simplicity of use.

An "ample of a program in this machine language,

which takes 16 instructions and 28 16-bit words of memory storage, to read in one thousand numbers, store them in consecutive memory locations, sum them, and print out the sum. However, please note that the English description of what the program does (though much easier to say and comprehend) itself requires 103 characters, each equivalent to 8 bits; so that it is almost twice as long as the machine-language program. Indeed, the difficulty of the latter lies not in its length, but in its alien and opaque form of expression of what it does. The first improvement on machine language was assembly language. This is not very different from machine language, but removes the most glaring and trivial irritations. First, instructions may be labelled, so that one no longer needs to count lines to address jump instructions; *one jumps to the label*. This is also a great help when one wishes to insert additional instructions, either to correct or modify a program (every jump need not be changed). Second, memory may be labelled, so that numbers may be stored in symbolic addresses and retrieved therefrom, leaving it to a computer program to assign actual storage. Third, the entire program becomes *relocatable* anywhere in the computer memory. Finally, and perhaps more trivially, the op-codes may be replaced by abbreviated mnemonics, and the instruction layout may be relaxed, using punctuation marks. Of course, a program written in assembly language is no longer directly intelligible to the computer or executable by it. It becomes a piece of textual input, to a "translator program" called the assembler. Naturally, the program may be stored in the computer's memory, like any other piece of text; but, before it can be executed, it must be "assembled." The assembler finds appropriate space for the object code (i.e. the machine language equivalent of the input program) and for its needed storage space (often called variables). The assembly language instructions correspond, one-to-one, to machine-language instructions.

For example, we may denote memory locations by one, two, or three lower-case letters (both for labelling instructions and naming variables). A numerical address will still be allowed. Absolute addresses (i.e. actual numbers; d=O) will correspond to quoted numbers (e.g. "6000"); direct addresses (d=1) to variables named as stated; indirect addresses (d=2) to variable names placed in parentheses; and relative addresses will not be used "'With relocatable programs and symbolic addresses, they are no longer useful). Accumulators (X, Y, XY, or Z) will not be referred to symbolically, hut only by these names. Instruction labels will precede the instruction and will be terminated by a colon (:). Spaces will be ignored. Op-codes will be denoted by strings of capital letters and terminated by a comma (,), which will also separate multiple arguments.

A sample specification of assembly language op-codes is shown in figure 1. In the assembly language notation, A denotes X (a=0), Y (a= 1), XY (a=2), or Z (a=3). Italic letters (p, x, or b) denote numbers (possibly in quotes, to denote absolutes) or variables names (possibly in parentheses, to denote indirect addressing), and are interpreted according to the op-code (e.g. A cannot be XY in IN and OUT instructions; if A is XY in instructions with c = 1, 2, and 4 (with p □ 5), the operand must be 32 bits long-either a double-length number, or an address referring to the first of two consecutive 16-bit memory words. Again, the reader must remember that it is not the particular details of our specifications that are important or memorable but the kind and degree of detail occurring.

Assembly language mnemonic	Machine language instruction
IN **A**, (*p*-8)	$c = 0$, a □ 2, $p \geq 8$
OUT **A**, *p*	$c = 0$, a □ 2, $p \leq 7$
TO **A**, x	$c = 1$
FROM **A**, x	$c = 2$, $d \geq 1$

FROMA, B	$c = 2, d = 0$
CL, **A**	$c = 3, d = 0$
NEG **A**	$c = 3, d = 1$
NOT **A**	$c = 3, d = 2$
RNDx	$c = 3, d = 3$, a = 2
ADD **A**, x	$c = 4, p = 0$
SUB **A**, x	$c = 4, p = 1$ –
AND **A**, x	$c = 4, p = 2$ –
OR **A**, x	$c = 4, p = 3$
XOR **A**, x	$c = 4, p = 4$
LADD, x	$c = 4, p = 5$
LSUB, x	$c = 4, p = 6$
LAND, x	$c = 4, p = 7$
LOR, x	$c = 4, p = 8$
LXOR, x	$c = 4, p = 9$
CSHL **A**, P	$c = 5, d = 0$
CSHR **A**, P	$c = 5, d = 1$
ASHL **A**, P	$c = 5, d = 2$
ASHR **A**, P	$c = 5, d = 3$
JMP, x	$c = 6, p = 0$
JPCZ **A**, x	$c = 6, p = 1$
JPCNN **A**, x	$c = 6, p = 2$
JPCNZ **A**, x	$c = 6, p = 3$
JPCP **A**, x	$c = 6, p = 4$
JPCB **A**, 0, *b*, x	$c = 6, p = 5$
BIT **A**, 0, *b*	$c = 6, p = 6$
BIT **A**, 1, *b*	$c = 7, d = 1$
BITNOT **A**, *b*	$c = 7, d = 2$
STOP	$c = 8$
INTER	c = 9

Figure 1: Typical assembly language mnemonics

```
     CL X; FROM X, SUM; TOX, '5000'
ret: FROM X, W; SUB X '6000'; JPCZX, out
     INX, 1; FROM X, (W); ADD X, sum
     FROM X, sum
     TOX, W; ADD X, '1'; JP, ret
out: TO X, sum; OUT X, 2; STOP
```

Figure 2: The summation program in assembly language

Consider figure 2. Here, numbers are given in decimal notation. Note the tremendous improvement in direct legibility of the program in comparison with the binary strings. The assembler is left to figure out where to store the sum (the variable "sum" which the machine language program put into address 6000) and the current address of the listed numbers (the variable "w," which the machine language program puts at location 28 if the program begins at location 0, necessitating counting the words occupied by the program; if the program were to be modified or relocated, this would have to be changed, and would be an unnecessary source of programming errors); and similarly, there is no need to count words to determine the addresses of "ret" and "out" (placed by the machine language program at 5 and 24 ' as it happens). As an exercise, the readers may wish to try to modify the program so as to allow for the possibility that the sum of the 1000 numbers might occupy more than 16 bits. In machine language this requires no less than 12 changes and seven shifts of memory location.

In assembly language only the substantive changes (from the programmer's point of view) need be made. The amended program is given in figure 3. Here we note that only seven changes are needed; but observe that "sum"

```
     CL XY; FROM XY, SUM; TOX, '5000'
ret: FROM X, W; SUB X '6000'; JPCZX, out IN X, 1; FROM X, (W); TO
     XY, sum ADD XY, (w);
     FROM XY, sum  TO X,W; ADD X, '1'; JMP, ret
out: TO XY, sum; OUT X, 2; OUT Y, 2; STOP
(Underlined material represents changes from previous program).
Alternative version would have third line replaced by:
CLX; IN Y, 1, FROM Y, (W); LADD, sum FROM XY, sum
```

Figure 3: The summation program modified for long sums

becomes a double-length address-just another piece of bookkeeping handled automatically by the assembler.

Of course, a program in assembly language still represents, instruction-by-instruction, a program in machine language, and therefore still has the defects of "walking the road in extremely short steps," as we put it earlier.

All that shuffling of numbers in and out of the accumulators, counting and restricted testing, is not natural to us, and its mechanical nature suggests that an improvement is still possible. Thus it was not long before programmers devised much more humanly natural languages, which are generically called *higher-level* (or *algebraic*) *languages*. Some of the more common ones are ADA, ALGOL, APL, BASIC, C, COBOL, FORTRAN, LISP, PASCAL, PL/I, RPG-II, SNOBOL, SPITBOL, WATFOR, and WATFIV. There are more; and all come with a variety of versions and dialects.

The characteristic that puts a language into this class is that one higher-level instruction translates into several assembly or machine language instructions. Beyond this, the languages differ according to the kind of program they are intended for.

While most languages will perform most tasks, FORTRAN was clearly intended to do scientific and engineering computations, COBOL to perform business data-processing, LISP to manipulate lists, and SNOBOL, strings of text. As a final illustration of the power and intelligibility of such languages, we present higher-level versions of our summation program in BASIC, WATFIV, and PASCAL. Once more, note that the details of the individual languages do not matter to us at this point (though, if the reader ever intends to program, then some language will have to be thoroughly understood; but assume that many of my readers have no such intention); it is their general flavor and appearance that is noteworthy; and the casual readability of the samples presented is their salient characteristic.

Of all the hundreds of programming languages devised, it is safe to say that more lines of program have been written in FORTRAN or COBOL than in all others combined, though this reflects their age rather than their desirability. The fast-gaining runner-up must surely be BASIC, which comes with every micro- and most mini-computers; though some would say that BASIC, which perpetuates the Style of FORTRAN, spoils any chances of producing really good programs and should be replaced by PASCAL. Fashions come and go in programming languages, not always fully based on rational arguments, and personal preferences vigorously touted.

Given a higher-level language, it is necessary to have a translator program to turn it into machine (or more frequently assembly) language. Such translators are of two kinds.

An interpreter operates at execution time: beginning with the first instruction of the stored higher-level program, it translates it into one or more machine language instructions, which it proceeds to execute; then it reads and translates the next higher-level instruction and executes that; and so on. If a jump is encountered in the source program (as the higher-level language program is often called), the interpreter goes to the next instruction in accordance with the jump and proceeds to read, translate, and execute it, without taking into account whether it has already encountered it. Thus, the same source instructions will have to be parsed and translated a thousand times (a very time-consuming and wasteful procedure). But the (usually much longer) object program need not be stored, and interpreters themselves tend to be shorter and simpler programs. This is why a BASIC interpreter is a natural adjunct to a microcomputer, which tends to be a little cramped for space; especially since many microcomputer users are riot interested in extremely lengthy computations.

By contrast, a *compiler* is a program that translates a source program into an object program, the former being in higher-level language and the latter in machine or assembly language.

The program is translated as it sits in memory, not during execution; so that the problem of repeated translation is avoided. Indeed, there are many so-called "optimizing compilers" which pass through the compiled object code several times, eliminating redundancies and inefficiencies to produce faster object programs (something that would be impossible for an interpreter to do). Speed is greatly increased, in general, at the expense of space in the computer memory. Of course, once a program has been compiled and proven to be free of bugs (debugging is far easier in source code than in object code), the source program may be stored for future use and only the object program kept in main memory. Compilers are available for almost all higher-level languages on almost all machines, and are essential for extensive applications.

COMPUTER SOFTWARE

The programs, or software, available for computers fall into two classes, *system software* and roughly, the system software comprises those programs that are considered indispensable to the general operation of a given computer system, forming what is often termed the operating system of the computer, and generally are supplied by the manufacturer, though alternative operating systems are sometimes available from software houses; while the applications software includes all those programs that are needed by one computer user but not by another, even if such programs are widely required, and while some manufacturers will sell applications software (as optional additions to their systems), more often this is obtained from software specialists.

We begin with the *operating system*. This may be divided into a kernel of absolutely indispensable programs and a shell of almost indispensable, so-called utility programs. The kernel (or nucleus) is also sometimes termed the monitor. To understand why this kernel program is needed, we consider what happens when we type a character (say an "A") on our keyboard, as part of a message to the computer. Because our timescale recognizes perhaps 1/20 second, while the computer may deal in units of 1/1,000,000 second, if we want to type an "A" we may find ourselves actually transmitting some 50,000 A's to the computer, before our finger leaves the key! If the keyboard mechanism were to transmit the A for only one microsecond, on the other hand, the computer might well be busy elsewhere during this particular μs and miss it altogether. Therefore, it is necessary to establish a protocol (in the usual diplomatic sense, a formal structure for the orderly passage of information) or "handshaking" procedure. This is often done by sending the A on one line (or lines) and simultaneously sending a pulse along an auxiliary line, which sets a "flag" bit in the CPU. When the computer is ready to receive a new character, it checks the appropriate flag bit over and over, until it detects that it has been set. Then it reads the character, resets the flag to its "null" state, and sends a signal pulse back to the keyboard (or its controlling circuitry), telling it that the character has been received. The flag is always open, so the transmit pulse need only be sent once by the keyboard; but the character continues to be sent until it is acknowledged by the computer Thus a keyboard character will neither be missed nor read repeatedly. In addition, either the CPU or the keyboard controller should send the "A" to whatever device displays the typed characters.

If the particular keyboard were to be the only input device ever to be connected to the CPU, it would be best to incorporate all this in the circuitry of the cpu; but since there may be several different inputs to the CPU, and several types of terminal may be used, coming from different manufacturers, it is found preferable to have the I/O *procedures* made part of the operating system. In addition to the keyboard input already described, there will be short machine language programs for input from any other devices attached to the computer and corresponding programs for output to display screens, printers, and so on. The orderly operation of a computer is subject to interruptions (or *interrupts*, as they are known in Computerese), either because a program contains an instruction that at some point, is not executable (such as a division by zero or a reference to a nonexistent memory location), or because someone needs to terminate execution for some overriding reason (such as the decision that a program is in error and is generating garbage or is in an infinite loop). Handling errors and interrupts is another function of the kernel of the operating system, as is the start-up (or "bootstrap") procedure which initializes operation. If, as is often the case, several users are connected to the computer, then the operating system must handle the tasks of Job-scheduling (and Job accounting and billing, if this is appropriate), and the allocation of storage, in main and extended memory, and of other resources (such as printers or communication lines), and the management of *time-sharing* (as between several terminals). Another task that is handled by the operating system is the management of *user files*, and their transfer between main memory and extended memory (such as disk). Indeed, one sees frequent reference to *disk operating systems*, such is the importance of this function of the operating system.

Another function of the kernel is to provide protection and security to users and to itself, both from authorized users encroaching on forbidden territory and from unauthorized users attempting to use the computer.

Ideally, each user should, on giving the correct access code (such as a "password")—this feature did not exist on the first computers, and is still absent in personal microcomputers with only one user/owner-have access strictly limited to the parts of the computer allocated to him or her by the operating system, but in such a way that the impression is maintained that he or she is the only user present.

Another very congenial aspect of this concept is that some operating systems conduct their memory management function in such a way that the user need make no distinction between main and extended memory; this is referred to as a virtual memory system. The kernel program has to be able to display, move, modify, and search, at least the main memory, and to initiate execution at any given address, or activate any of the peripheral devices. Using these functions, by means of appropriate commands in the "operating system language," together with its file-handling capabilities, the system can load, compile, or execute any program stored in its memory (main or extended) written in machine, assembly, or higher-level language, provided that a suitable compiler or other translator is available to it.

We now turn to the utilities provided by most operating systems. First, we have an assembler (and perhaps also a *disassembler,* which translates a program written in machine language into the more intelligible assembly language; as well as a *macroassembler,* which allows the user to define his own macroinstructions in machine or assembly language), together with a selection of translation programs, either interpreters or compilers, for the higher-level languages that the user wishes to employ.

The smaller microcomputers will provide an

interpreter for some dialect Of BASIC, since this a relatively simple language to learn and to interpret into machine or assembly language; beyond this, one must pay for additional languages. There may also be a variety of TRACING and DEBUGGING utilities, according to the cost, size, and sophistication of the computer and its operating system.

There will be facilities for linking or chaining programs together. While the kernel will contain the rudiments of a file-handling system (to create, destroy, list, locate, and transfer files), there will also be utilities for further management of these. Such programs will sort, find (among other files), search (in a given file, for information specified), transform, edit, and combine files. Indeed, a good editor program can enormously facilitate the rapid and painless creation and modification of files, which include both text and programs.

The line separating the kernel from the shell of utilities is purely conceptual and far from sharp. Similarly, the boundary of the entire operating system is far from definite. What is available beyond the essentials mentioned above will be called part of any decent system by some, part of a compiled language by others, and just applications software by still others, depending on their point of view. The ability to handle a variety of data structures (such as arrays, lists, strings of characters, trees, queues, and stacks) may come from the use of a suitable higher-level language or from an extended "system development" utility package.

Similarly, languages intended for scientific and engineering applications usually handle floating-point and multiple-precision arithmetic, though this may be provided even in computer hardware. The same applies to routines for computing, for example, sines, cosines, logarithms, etc., and pseudorandom numbers (the last beloved of computer games inventors!)

A *data-base management system* (DBMS) may be just a glorified file-handling utility; or may be an elaborate program, cross-indexed and relational, with its own language of special commands, for answering any conceivable question about a large amount of intricately structured data.

As is often the case, you gets what you pays for, both in money and in memory space; and vendors' claims have to be carefully scrutinized and verified. It is advisable not to overbuy one's capabilities beyond one's needs.

Similarly, a graphics package may simply allow one to produce passable graphs, histograms (i.e. bar-graphs), pie-charts, and perhaps games, with a resolution of some 200 by 300 delightfully named pixels; or it may allow you to resolve perhaps 2000 by 3000 pixels, in a variety of colors, with the ability to draw complex three-dimensional shapes, properly shaded, illuminated, and textured, and move them by commands in a special language. The latter systems are a lot of fun to operate, and can be most helpful to draughtsmen, animators, film designers, and simulator-trainer designers; but they cost a bundle, and they require quite powerful computers to hold and run them.

Another offshoot of the file handier is a cluster of programs for generating *reports, journal ledgers,* and *accounts* of all kinds, as well as forms and mailing' lists (the latter leading to a kind of DBMS in which mailing lists are matched to interests and characteristics of the individuals itemized).

Again, there are statistical packages of various degrees of sophistication, from a mean-variance-covariance calculator, to systems able to analyse very complex sets of data by elaborate techniques, using a whole statistical computer language. What has been described as "the most popular program ever written" is usually given the generic name of an *electronic worksheet,* though the trade name of the first such program, Visi-Calc, like Kleenex and Vaseline, has become almost generic.

A table is presented on the video screen and each entry is allocated either a numerical value or a formula relating it to other entries. When the data are sufficient, the resulting numbers are displayed. When an entry is changed, it and all entries depending on it are altered accordingly at once. This provides a representation of a given situation surpassed only by a graph in its impact, and a first-class planning aid. Finally, among the borderline system/applications software utilities, will put what is usually called a word-processing package (though would prefer either character or text processor). This is an extension of an editing utility, in which the text may by "scrolled" up and down on the screen, edited in the usual ways, but also more specifically for producing letters, articles, reports, and other written copy.

Margins may be set and the text right, left, or double justified, or set up in multi-column pages, with page numbering, indexing, and even the use of different sizes and styles of typeface, in the most sophisticated systems. Here again, cost rises steeply, and one should buy only what one will need.

Beyond these programs, there lies an endless variety of unquestionable applications programs. There are programs for ballistics, boat design, analysis of molecular structure from x-ray diffraction data, tabulation of Bessel functions, simulation of naval battles and economic cycles, etc.

Most of these are not on the market and only work on one machine; but there are very many programs available on the open market, produced or distributed by software houses, with various levels of efficiency, sophistication, and *Programming* is a fascinating, intricate, rewarding, but unforgiving and at times infuriating occupation. We will encourage all of you who have the time to try it. If you have a computer at your disposal, it would be a shame not to learn a simple language, such as BASIC or PASCAL and try your hand at writing a simple program or two. The sense of achievement when you have a working program is great; perhaps because the process is addictive and consumes much more time than you would believe possible.

2

What is Information?

Information is one of those misunderstood concepts. Yet it is at the same time one of the most used. We go to the bus station to seek information from timetables. We obtain information from government offices such as the DSS and the DVLC. Banks, supermarkets, leisure centres, libraries and even the police ply us with more. Newspapers, television and the radio present us with their own ideas of what information should be. In many instances, however, we may not agree with their conclusions. McLeod termed its subjectivity as being one person's junk and another's treasure.

We all understand and deal with this accordingly when extracting news from the media, for example. Yet many of our organizations consider information to be something more. They see it as a vital resource, to be managed like any other valuable resource. How it is used and disseminated through the available technology can determine how efficient, and indeed effective, an organization is. Peter Drucker sees information acquired in a systematic and purposeful way as enhancing an organization's productivity.

Information is important, we cannot operate without it. But more than this, we are discovering that our ability to process it by increasingly sophisticated technological means is fundamentally changing the way that employees perceive their organizational environment. The consequences of this could be either to break down established functional controls or indeed to enhance them by becoming super-efficient. Much will depend upon the characteristics of the organization before implementation.

As firms become increasingly 'information dependent' we need to identify the perceptual relationship between ourselves and the information we use. How, for instance, can we possibly design an adequate information system if we do not understand the nature of information? The answer to this lies, in part, with the conventional wisdom of the day. Managers, like everybody else, develop their views through exposure to established ideas. Thus the way in which they understand information will influence the way in which they treat it. Such conventional wisdom is coloured by the technicians on the one hand and the user's own experience on the other.

Anecdotal prescriptions abound as guidelines to the way forward for all who care to listen. These arise from a blanket of professional and academic thinking which surrounds the business environment and provides remedies for action. We could categorize all these ideas into two bodies of thought, two paradigms. The first could be termed the resource-driven paradigm. This is because its central theme in understanding information is the continuity and consistency of the information itself. It is very much in vogue at present.

The second body of thought is the perception-driven paradigm. Information is seen as an abstract concept, the product of individual perception. It is a temporary phenomenon and as such belongs only to the receiver. The difference is not merely one of academic debate. Managements adopting one or the other can affect the design of their organizations. If information is considered to be a resource then resulting systems are usually more centrally controlled, the assumption being that all information is corporate property. Whereas information considered to be personally owned is seen as being outside the formal structure.

Within the framework of this paradigm the view of information is coloured by its use as a resource. Like any other resource it can be tapped at any time with the certainty of achieving a predictable value from it. Information is regarded as unchanging, and therefore can be easily accommodated into a firm's formal procedure. There is a range of propositions available which seeks to explain information. Each proposition has a consequence for organizational design. Listed below are those major themes and what their implications might be on business.

Herbert A. Simon took the view that information, along with energy, constitute the two basic currencies of our society. We need energy to breathe, to move, to think, to live. But this alone is not enough. We need to know when to breathe, when to move and how to think. Information provides us with that knowledge. To adopt this perspective is to interpret information as an independent entity. It is all about us waiting to picked up and used. There may be minor variations in its interpretation by different individuals, but consistency can be easily achieved through better training.

Specific sets of information, such as finance information, are given a unique value by organizations which is usually based upon departmental rather than individual need. Particular information is thus attached to particular departments. This allows information to be generally accessible because perceptions of it are bound by the formal departmental framework. Information is then tied into that framework and cannot be used legitimately within any other context, thus guarding its consistency. What is excluded, therefore, is an important role for the individual receiver. This is not to suggest that information cannot be perceived by individuals. Psychologists such as Anderson and Bower have long been aware of the importance of information reception in determining an individual's behaviour.

However, information can be received automatically without an individual having to understand it. For example, through training an employee could process production statistics without knowing what they mean. In this case it is the functional process (through its formal procedure) that is acting as the receiver rather than the individual. An accounting process, for instance, responds to specific inputs without anyone having to understand them. A motor car responds to certain information transmitted through mechanisms such as the throttle, steering wheel or brake. Both of these examples are designed to act as receivers to specific information.

By implication, information can be transmitted to any receiver that logs into the particular transmission. In the same way as a radio picks up a station when it is switched on, the right form will pick up the right information. And like radio waves, information is omnipresent, only needing the correct tuning. Such a view allows information the continuity and consistency required to be regarded as a resource. It also allows a further proposition.

The design of any formal information system must assume that information does not change during transmission. It can, however, be transformed from data or other information sets before transmission. Within such a framework it is the transmitting functions (departments, processes, etc.) which are considered to be the main determinants. The information receiving functions (also departments, processes, etc.) are designed to link into the operational needs of the transmitter functions.

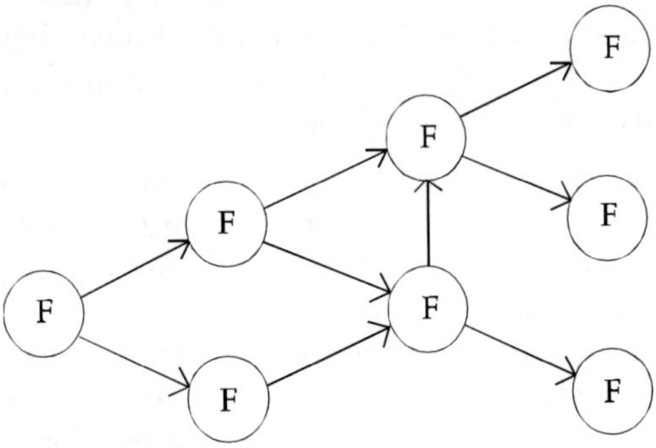

F = functions

Fig. 1. An information network between functions

Each function, however, can be both transmitter and receiver of information, and together with other functions will form part of a integrated network. The functions are tied by their simultaneous roles as information receivers and transmitters, thereby being prevented as much as possible from deviancy in their information usage.

Consequence. Business organizations are driven by those functions which transmit information. The higher the value that a particular set of information is given, the more important will be its relating transmitter function. For example, the finance department could both transmit and receive information. Indeed, each job function within that department could also do the same. A cost clerk, for instance, receives information from the factory floor which he then processes into other information and transmits to some other source, perhaps management. The value of the information he processes will depend upon the utility his organization has placed upon it. If the utility is high, then the prestige attached to the transmitting function will also be high irrespective of job complexity. In the same way, if a department has a great number of important information transmitters within its control, then it too will be prestigious and possess influence. Why certain sets of information are prestigious and others are not will depend, amongst other things, upon the organization's political processes.

PERCEPTION-DRIVEN PARADIGM

The perception-driven paradigm does not consider information to be a resource. Individuals or groups are seen to own their information. What belongs to the organization are the data sets, the facts and figures specific to certain functions. For instance, data on how an organization is performing in its market quite obviously belong to that firm. How well that data is used is dependent upon the individual's own competence in interpreting it. Management can control this indirectly through training, but they cannot directly control the thought processes which turns data into information. Once again, there is a collection of propositions or ideas about information which formulate a general approach.

Adherence to this paradigm, as in the previous paradigm, may not necessarily be by conviction but rather by default because people not treating information as a resource automatically form part of this group. However, there are others who are members by conviction. Information is said to be receiver-dependent in that any set of information can be considered to be information only if it is recognised as having value by a particular individual. Thus a river flooding may be information to someone who lives on its banks but of no consequence to someone living several miles away.

It would be difficult, therefore, to understand information as group or organization property since its determination is subjective. Management teams have implemented computer technology and in so doing also developed their information sets into a resource. They experience problems, usually some time after a successful launch, and then abandon using their technology in an integrative manner, returning to the 'islands' approach (that is, a computer system, perhaps physically integrated through networks, etc. but perceptually segregated into different functional areas). Information is no longer seen as a resource; indeed its treatment as such is often seen as the culprit and not the technology itself.

Both paradigms recognize a difference between data and information. Computer personnel, for example, have long known of the distinction. Information is seen by them as processed data. The two are interrelated, data being the input to a process, and information the output. In the same way that an output of one system can form the input of another, information from one system can form the data of another. This is consistent with treating information as a resource. Perceptually-conceived information on the other hand is not the consequence of a formalized process. Data are a factor, but then so are other aspects such as individual traits, culture, structure and political processes.

The relationship between data and information is, therefore, not so strong. sThis contradicts the objectives implied by the creation of management information systems and data processing. The former allows the individual access to established information, whilst the latter converts data into information. Since the production of information cannot be formalized there is no point in trying to achieve it. Systems should, therefore, be designed to produce the most accurate and readable data in order to enhance easy conversion into information.

When Ligomenides describes information as a fundamental force, he should be referring to data. Levitan, on the other hand, is correct in claiming information to be dynamic and continuously evolving. The logic of these two views can be seen when data and information are differentiated. It is only data which is time-independent, and therefore unchanging and static—a fundamental force. By this we mean that data retains a constant empirical value: a fact is a fact and cannot be altered. Information, on the other hand, can be altered and changed. It is time-dependent and thus its value can alter from one moment to the next. It is dynamic and evolving because it is determined by an individual's perception.

It is, indeed, time and utility which transform data into information. If at a particular time a set of data is useful to an individual then it can be described as information. Equally, at another time the same set of data may not have utility and therefore not be information. The data themselves have not changed in any way, remaining always constant. What has changed is the individual's perception of those data. Information is in reality the consequence of a complex psychological process which transforms perceived data into usable thought inputs.

It is, therefore, data which the individual receives from the environment, the brain which transforms these data into information. No formal system can directly pre-empt this stage; thus no formal system can transform data into information.

Data can be transformed into different data, transmitted and received. For example, production data submitted to the cost department and processed into second generation costed production data, which are in turn submitted to the financial director. Information is transformed, in part, from data; it can only be received and never transmitted. The financial director may attach value to costed production data and thus receive it as information. If he/she passes it on, it will once again be as data, perhaps refined into third generation data. There cannot be information systems because information is so transient.

The individual's subjectivity, which can be developed by training and formal procedure, determines what is information. At another time that perception may be different. Information systems cannot work in this way. Their assumption must be that information is not transient but consistent.

Quite obviously information systems do exist in one form or another. They may not be what they claim to be but they are nevertheless working. Is it worth arguing the difference? The answer to that lies within ourselves. Our actions and behaviour, and consequently our organizations, are governed by our perceptions. If, therefore, we understand information to be permanent rather than transient then how we organize ourselves will be coloured by that. We will design systems which use information as a resource and expect it to be totally consistent.

STRUCTURAL IMPLICATIONS

The difference between these two paradigms may seem subtle, and in terms of information usage it may well be. However, NBS research indicates that the effects upon organizational design can be major. Structural characteristics consequent upon individually-owned information, for instance, can adopt two extremes. On the one hand they can be organic and informal (adhocracies) whereby all members are seen as contributing equally, each possessing a particular range of techniques to interpret data, whilst at the other extreme there are formal and mechanistic organizations (bureaucracies). The rigidities of structure stifle any use of information as a resource, so by default such processes are left to the individual. These contrast with the resource-driven paradigm in which the structural characteristics of organizations are seen to be centrally orientated, with spheres of influence at the periphery, their importance dependent upon the perceived value of particular sets of information.

THE WIDER IMPLICATIONS OF INFORMATION

The development of an organization orientated toward the resource-driven concept of information is well known, and many large firms are aligned in that direction. A sophisticated network is established, more than likely computerized, accessing and distributing information. Particular attention is paid to ensuring standardization of information sets. For example, a piece of costing information is so devised that it can be used by accounts, marketing and production. These organizations treat all information as their property, attaching to it a value like any other asset. This denies the employee any sense of ownership and tends to detach them from the work process with consequential inefficiencies evolving. It is asserted, that a motivated staff is a contented and efficient staff.

One important way to motivate is to give the individual responsibility within their job. Such responsibility is manifest in how much ability a person will be given to determine the information need of their particular function. To standardize information in the way that many corporate systems do, takes away that fundamental element of responsibility. Levitan, on the other hand, would claim this to be an inevitable consequence of increasingly sophisticated corporate structures. In addition, Karen Levitan and others imply that information which is not used as a resource is inferior. On the contrary, one could argue that giving the individual ownership could result in a greater entrepreneurial drive.

Standardization is the killer of innovation. It is difficult to conceive of any substantial organization, however, where such a degree of individuality could be tolerated. Their size demands a need for cohesion through standardized practice. Therefore it is only in the smaller establishments where such freedom would work. Large organizations which do not treat their information as a resource still exist. Their mechanisms of control, however, are not informal or organic. Indeed, the realities are the converse. Individuality is stifled by greater control, rather than less. No-one is trusted to use information for the organization's good without formal control procedures. Classic examples of such organizations are to be found within the civil service or large quasi-government institutions such as the post office.

It has been suggested that there is a relationship between the way in which a firm uses its information and its structure. A matrix can be established differentiating organizations in terms of how they treat their information and the consequential structural characteristics. If, for example, information is plotted against size (another important contingent of organization) four major structural types could be identified. Each is the outcome of the way a particular firm uses its information.

On the vertical axis of the matrix are the two extremes of information. On the horizontal axis are the two extremes of organizational size. Both information and size are considered to be contingents, that is variables which affect the characteristics of an organization. The four possible combinations of these two variables determine four organizational structures. Thus each structure is an ideal for each of the four combinations. For example, a managerial structure is the appropriate structure for a large firm using information as a resource.

Treatment of information	Large	Small
Resource	Managerial	Technical/ professional
Perception	Bureaucratic	Entrepreneurial

Structure parameters:
Managerial: larger in size with central/top control but with more departmental integration
Bureaucratic: larger in size with formal structure and a diversified control
Technical/professional: smaller in size with a professional body and formal structure
Entrepreneurial: centrally controlled but with less formal structure and smaller in size

Fig. 2. Information/structure matrix

Research into the validity of such a matrix is by no means complete. There is evidence from the NBS regional survey, for example, that such a correlation does indeed exist. In general, the more successful managerial-style firms tend to treat their information as a resource, whilst the more successful entrepreneurial organizations tend to treat their information as a perceptual phenomenon, and so on. It is not yet certain whether the matrix is predictive, that is implying combinations which are not successful. There is sufficient evidence, however, to support the claim that information usage affects organizational structure.

The issue of information is much more than whether or not it is a resource. Information is indeed the essence of an organization, shaping and determining its structure.

For example, bureaucratic organizations could hot effectively treat information as a resource because their mechanisms could not control it that way. A technical/ professional organization, on the other hand, is better able to handle its information as a resource because of its structural characteristics.

The implication is that there should be a natural balance between the design of an organization and its information structure. Where this has not been achieved it is because managers are not matching the structure of their organizations with an appropriate usage of information. NBS research has also shown that the implementation of computer technology can worsen any potential for imbalance. This is perhaps because of two factors.

Firstly, the characteristics of the technology itself do tend to enhance resource-driven rather than perception-driven information. Secondly, the greater volume of information generated makes the problem more apparent.

If the matrix in Figure 2 is valid then there is neither a right nor a wrong way to control information: much depends upon the individual circumstances. Resource-driven information and perception-driven information are opposite extremes of one continuum.

Management teams were grasping eagerly at the new computer technology as a solution to their efficiency problems. There were at that time forces in the environment—market, political, social or economic—with which the traditional methods of organization could not cope; it was believed that the computer would provide all the answers. In the space of that time many colleagues began to discover that the impact of computer technology seemed to be contradictory. On the one hand, it did tend to improve efficiency, whilst on the other it was not always so certain that an improvement in effectiveness followed. It seemed that underlying, and as yet not understood, forces were at work.

Departments employing the same technology were more or less successful than others. Business organizations with all the ingredients of success and implementing computers to further fuel their growth quite often experienced failure a few years later. Since those early days there has been considerable discussion and research on the impact of information technology. It seemed that the perceptual aspects of organization were not merely misunderstood but often ignored, and thus we were not able to understand fully the implications of introducing information technology. We now realize that not only does it have an impact on the way we run organizations, it also has an impact on our behaviour. There is a readily understood physical aspect of any firm and a more abstract, perceptual aspect which arises from the way that people behave as a collective. Information technology is not the only agent in this process, but because of its particular characteristics it can have an extraordinarily powerful effect on both these aspects. One of two main objectives of this book, therefore, is to underline the importance of the relationship between information technology (and to a lesser extent general technology) and its organizational structure.

The two are inseparable. Models that seek to understand either technology or organization must do so within the framework created by this relationship. Otherwise an essential factor leading to an appropriate analysis will be missed. The other main objective is to produce a model which can do this. Unlike many of its predecessors, the model will not concentrate -on the functional or hierarchical nature of organizations but rather on the dichotomy between the physical and perceptual aspects. This exists whether or not there is information technology present, but in many cases the implementation of such technology can exacerbate potential dysfunctional forces existing between the two. In effect there are two organizations—a physical organization and a perceptual or virtual organization.

The impact that information technology can have on the sometimes tenuous relationship existing between the two can be quite profound. The model explores thoroughly this relationship. It proposes virtual organization as the antithesis of physical organization. That is abstract, unseeing and existing within the minds of those who form a particular organization. The point being that because the framework of virtual organization is often subjective and open to many different perceptual interpretations, it is difficult for anyone to establish an appropriate response to it. This makes it no less real; nor does it reduce the need to respond to it. Left unattended the effects of virtual organization can be quite catastrophic, especially if stimulated by the impact of information technology. This has considerable significance for the practitioner, especially those who have introduced, or are thinking of introducing, information technology. The model suggests that for a firm to survive there would ideally exist a dynamic equilibrium between the two organizations which has been termed the organizational balance. Anything which upsets this balance, such as the introduction of information technology, has to be compensated for by proactive action of management. If managers do not understand, nor indeed perceive the existence of virtual organization, then they will not be able take the appropriate measures. Long-term structural weaknesses or even total failure of the business can result.

Demonstrating the existence of virtual organization can be problematic. By definition it cannot be observed directly since it exists only in the mind. At best one could ask a selection of staff for their impressions and make certain deductions, but these are likely to be dubious and tainted with the researcher's own perceptions. As such there has deliberately been no direct empirical research to establish the foundations of this model. Support for its validity has been sought in three other areas. Firstly, there is indirect empirical data gained from several research projects conducted at the Newcastle Business School. This comprises a study over two years by Stuart Maguire and myself into eighty-five small to large firms in all sectors of the North East. We examined particularly the strategy that firms employed to implement and control their information technology.

The data were gathered through a series of observations, interviews and involvement in the process. Other data were obtained from one or two firm studies on the impact of information technology by a group within the Newcastle Business School called AMBIS (Advanced Manufacturing and Business Information Systems). The argument for using these data rather than dedicated data is that they should be less contrived. Secondly, there is support to be gained from relevant personal experience. Although many would find this approach invalid because it does not comply with traditional or conventional ideas about research data, there is an increasing acceptance that such data can prove useful. In the social sciences, for example, Duke argued that such an approach (amongst others) would make a valuable contribution to the understanding of social experience. It is accepted that it cannot provide the only data, but the data that it does provide should be considered no less valid than any other.

We return to a more traditional style in support of the main arguments. That is, rather than gathering empirical evidence first and then developing a model, we should develop the model first from experiential instincts and then support it with data. This is put forward in the belief that to pursue the traditional methods of data-first research would not produce the generic model necessary to achieve the objectives set above. We have become unimaginative in our ideas about organization because we have been blinkered by too many sets of data.

How the book is structured in terms of presenting a logical argument takes on a greater significance than if it were based merely upon direct empirical data. It requires presentation of basic argument, counter-argument and a compromise position which leads the reader forward to the logical conclusion. This is the dialectic which involves thesis, antithesis and synthesis.

This overview, therefore, should not only cover the background to the book's major arguments and supportive material, but also provide the reader with a basic chapter plan.

To explain the impact of information technology we must look beyond the functional aspects of business organizations. The importance of information is reflected in its ability, through the appropriate technology, to corrupt departmental boundaries. This chapter, therefore, proposes that it is better to understand an organization as a network of information flows, which is itself set within other network flows of region, market, industry and so on. Such a perspective is underlined by many firms accessing information beyond their established functional boundaries. Within the organization, this could involve different departments accessing a common pool of information from the company database.

Externally, employees can gain entrance to public databases such as Prestel, which are run by autonomous bodies. The drive is towards centralization and hence better management control. Paradoxically, the opposite is being encouraged, whereby every user has the potential to access information which enables them to operate more efficiently, and also to do so outside the control of their manager. Under these conditions it is difficult for managers to control not only who reads and writes what but also, and perhaps more importantly, who knows what.

Large amounts of information can be processed and communicated via a network without managers ever being able to determine whether it runs contrary to their own policy. Security has, as a consequence, become an extremely important issue. The more the dissemination of information is allowed, the more likely control mechanisms will become corrupted.

In simple terms, data are facts, whilst information is the consequence of interpretation. What is information to some is not to others, and it is the subjective interpretation of what is and is not valuable which has caused managements considerable problems. The control parameters on the organization's database are based upon managers' own perceptions of its value as information which may not coincide with that of a potential intruder or misuser. But more than this, individual employees' perception of their information stock widens because of their greater accessibility to the information network. As a consequence, their perception of their own job parameters also widens beyond what management might think desirable.

WHAT IS INFORMATION TECHNOLOGY?

In so far as control over information forms the basis of managerial authority, the technologies which process it are inherently political. Indeed, business organizations are under pressure to change their decision-making structures as a direct consequence of information technology implementation. These 'subversive' effects on organizational structures are not immediately obvious to management. They arise as the new technology changes established work practices and consequently creates different relationships on the organization's information network. Management is then faced with a dual threat:

1. A new pool of knowledge outside its formal control structures. Employees are able to access information without hindrance.

2. Power is shifting from line managers to those who, control the information technology, such as the technicians in the DP departments or knowledgeable users.

Management's response has been weak and incremental. The control of information generated by computer technologies increasingly reflected the new power structures that these technologies established. On the one hand, functional control (allocation, budget, etc.) remains with general management. On the other, operational control (how and what is processed) is left to the technicians in the DP departments. The pervasive nature of the technology spreading through all levels of the organization established those who controlled it as important powerbrokers or gatekeepers. Newcastle Business School research has shown that senior managers are often unwilling to become involved. They served their apprenticeship in computerless or, at best, early mainframe-driven organizations and therefore do not always fully understand or appreciate the new technologies. Despite the obvious need for new control structures the traditional methods are adhered to.

The dichotomy between the established management structures and the changed (and changing) technological structures is therefore maintained and often worsened. Such opposing forces create a complex environment and place considerable constraints on management action. The dichotomy quickly becomes institutionalized. Lack of management action causes other user employees to perceive themselves as powerless in any dealings with the new technologies. This serves to enhance the influence of the technicians and is built into the organization's structures. Business action then tends to become increasingly inflexible; user managers are reluctant to take risks in an environment they do not understand, and many operational decisions are left to the technicians. This area of decision-taking is also built into the firm's task structure. Meanwhile the new networked systems demand increasing flexibility in order to work but are instead being faced with increasingly inflexible and decision-shy managements.

To appreciate the nature of this threat and how profound its impact can be on the organization, it is essential to grasp the characteristics of technology, in particular its integrative nature with any social entity whether it be an organization or something else. Explores this area, but it also then distinguishes between different types of technology, highlighting the perceptual characteristics of information technology. It concludes that to control information technology we must realize that we cannot treat it as just another piece of machinery.

The relationship between technology and an organization has, indeed, been thoroughly explored. It is obvious that a firm's structure is characterized by the many forces emanating from its operating environment. What is perhaps not so obvious is that technology is one of those forces. This is because it is quite often seen as a locally owned, physical resource. The machine on the shopfloor is just that and not part of a more complex social process. Within the framework of this perspective technology is a tool, totally predictable and controllable by management.

The physical technology alone (e.g. machinery or computers) will not explain how organizations are affected by it. As Weizenbaum suggested, a computer or telecommunication system (or any form of technology) is merely junk without the people to relate to them. It is how those people relate to their technology, how they use it, their perceptions of it and so on, that are important. These aspects govern not only the technological process but also the characteristics of the organization structure. In the same way, structure should not be seen merely in a physical sense. The dividing of a firm into departments and functions, although of interest, does not capture the essence of an organization, which is to be found within the minds of its employees. The relationship between technology and structure is thus not physical but perceptual because it is within people's minds that the links are made. Our understanding of such techno- behavioural forces is not great. This is partly because of the hegemonic view of business organizations as hierarchies in organization theory. It would seem, therefore, that we have not as yet learnt to examine organizations in an appropriate dimension which can highlight the effects of information and its technology.

The traditionalist's view of an organization is typically presented by Schein as a rational co-ordination of activities. This emphasizes the hierarchical and functionally-bound aspects. Butler, on the other hand, discussed the lack of understanding of such models determining that all the interrelationships are not adequately identified. They tend to portray firms as static entities without the turbulence of opposing forces. In particular, technology is seen as a side issue, if at all, and not central to the fundamental mechanisms of an organization.

A more appropriate model in Butler's mind is Udy's, which puts technology at the centre of an interactive environment of production objectives, social setting, physical exigencies and work organization. Technology, not the structure, sets the constraints ('trade-offs' as Butler calls them) upon an organization. Thus a certain structure can be considered suitable for a given technology. For example, a company using mass production techniques, such as Ford, will best be structured to suit the needs of mass production technology. The relationship does not end there, however, as in Pugh's model, because he suggests that it is technology which drives the organization.

Where this model fails is in not identifying with sufficient clarity the perceptual aspects of an organization's technology. It is only within this domain that useful links can be established between technology and structure. The perceptual aspects of structure must also be emphasized for this to be successful since within any physical domain technology can only be seen as a resource and structure as a functional framework. It will then demonstrate that employees' perception of their structure determines the consequent structural characteristics. This chapter also suggests, however, that the relationship is two-way, in that an established structure can itself influence and change the perception of the employees. The impact of information technology is then again introduced. Already have established that such technology can change the way that individuals perceive their environments. A link with the present chapter is that since an employee's perception of the environment can be changed through information technology, his/her perception of the firm's structure must also change. The post-implementation structure that emerges may be profoundly different from any previous structure.

This control-theoretic view of information technology's impact is particularly relevant to the devolution of management authority. The impact of the new technology may radically affect the power structure or the political relationships between management and staff (but not the functional relationships) thus creating an imbalance between the perceptual and physical aspects of the organization. Through the perceptual domain, information technology has also infiltrated the cultural base of organizations and has thus had the potential to alter cultural objectives, which are the consequence of existing value systems. For example, it may be the formal objective of one firm to produce good quality products at the expense of higher profits. This objective has arisen from the organization's culture, but any form of technology, especially information technology, is not sensitive to cultural requirements.

Managers may try to fit the technology into their companies but it is generally within a framework provided by the physical domain. The objectives suitable for the technology do not always match existing cultural needs. To seek an explanation of the technological impact, therefore, we should no longer look at organizations in terms of departments and divisions. Any boundary established by such a definition may be rendered irrelevant. It is more sensible to consider an organization as a network of perceptual maps, dependent on an information network which is itself part of a wider network within the region, market, industry and so on.

The need for such an outlook is underlined by the number of firms accessing information beyond their established functional boundaries. Internally, this involves different departments accessing a common pool from the company database; externally, employees gaining entrance to public databases such as Prestel. It is increasingly difficult to understand these organizations as physically controllable entities. The problem, however, extends beyond management. If it is accepted that our models of organization are also too limiting because of their inability to highlight the dichotomy between the perceptual and the physical, then we must develop new models, which is one of the major proposals of the book. In order to do this we must first establish an appropriate methodology. The analysis which must be pursued is wide- ranging. It extends beyond the convenient boundaries that traditional theory has established. The tidy logic of an organization reaches only into the physical domain, beyond that is a vast perceptual arena which can be understood only as a network of relationships.

THE DYNAMIC ELEMENT

Before its presentation, however, there are other factors which must be addressed. The point has already been made that an organization is a fluid and ever-changing entity. The components so far discussed form the framework of the organization but they are no more than boxes in an analyst's model. Other forces exist which breathe life into these concepts. They can be termed as the dynamics of an organization. People are the organization, and as such their perceptions, aspirations, alliances and conflicts form an important dynamic. It suggests that the outcome for any organization is not through a rational process, although that may seem to be apparent within the physical domain, but rather as a consequence of perceptual interaction between individuals or groups. These can be dysfunctional as well as functional.

For managers the issue is how such diverse forces can be controlled. They can only directly access the physical domain and therefore have to attempt to manipulate this in some way to have any impact upon the perceptual domain. One area, however, which allows a controllable linkage between the two domains is the information network. The quality, quantity and content of information, amongst other factors such as historicity, will determine an individual or group perception. On the other hand, the network itself can be physically manipulated thus affecting the quality, quantity and content of information. Its control is therefore of considerable importance to management.

Its particular emphasis is on the use of computer technology to generate information. Other forms of generated information through manual methods can also be controlled as information management, but because of the computer's ability to generate so much information other important forces come into play which are not present in a manual system.

The ways in which employees regard the characteristics of their information will determine in part the nature of their information network and ultimately the organization structure itself. Management must be aware of this and develop strategies through training and computer technology implementation which are sensitive to this. Information, however, is only part of the process. On its own it is not particularly a dynamic of the organization. Individuals may receive information and do nothing with it. A firm, therefore, does not change because of information. Information must be used. Action or behaviour is the consequence of information being used in the physical domain. In the perceptual domain, information being used is manifest through the decision process. There are no actions without decisions, no matter how minor or simple they may be, so that an organization, which can be analysed in terms of its actions, is driven by its decision processes.

In any context there is no such thing as an individual decision, even if the person involved is on a deserted island. Especially within a complex social process such as an organization, a decision is based upon a range of perceptual and physical influences. A person's experience coming to bear in a decision, for example, is the consequence of previous interactions with other people and institutions. Therefore one cannot fully control the decision process by controlling those individuals who are seen to own it. Their actions might be constrained but the source of their decisions is to be found in the perceptual domain. This is particularly important when such processes are affected by computer technology. Managers tend to develop mechanisms around the physical aspects of the technology and ignore the wider perceptual impact. It then places these ideas in the context of the other major components of a firm, in particular the information network, by highlighting the close relationship between a decision and information.

We have so far developed the framework of an organizational structure dominated by two domains: the physical and the perceptual. In a similar fashion to matter and anti-matter, their forces conflict and contradict one another. Management must maintain the narrow ground between the two, because it is only here that long-term stability is established. At this point the forces of both domains are in equilibrium, which for the purposes of the model has been termed balance. The achievement of such a state is one of the key outcomes to be identified.

The domination of one domain over another could lead to long-term instability, the degree of which depends upon a range of factors unique to specific organizations. For example, if there is no balance and an organization is dominated by its physical domain, then its short-term survival, at least, will depend upon how effective that domain is in dealing with the firm's particular environment. In the longer term, however, all firms must achieve an equilibrium whether the dominant domain is in tune with the environment or not. This is because the cost of not achieving equilibrium will be manifest in the dysfunctional relationship between the two domains. Forces will come into play that will undermine stability. It shows a complex social entity driven by an abstract relationship between two sets of forces. Much of this arena exists within the minds of the employees, of course, but like other societal phenomena its logic extends beyond them.

The forces can exist independently of particular individuals in that they are perpetuated by culture, technology and training. Individuals may come and go, some people may contribute more than others, but the logic of the organization as a separate entity remains consistent. It is proposed that an, organization can pass a significant point, the virtuality point, whereby its survival does not depend upon a particular set of individuals. This is a different world from the one portrayed by established theory. It comprises many of the same elements, such as structure and technology, recognized by conventional wisdom, but it is the perspective, the way in which those elements are arranged, that is different.

The emphasis is upon a force field relationship rather than the aspects of one domain or another. By having this different framework, we can also analyse the effects of change in other ways. In particular, the impact of information technology is shown to have a far wider effect upon organizations than the traditional models may lead us to suppose. Much of it is common sense, gleaned from the working environment and from those in it. Nevertheless, the model is placed before all management as a challenge: to use the ideas this book presents as a basis for analysing the worth of their information technology.

3

Organisation and Structure

The explanation of organizational structure was left to two mainstream approaches. The first was the economic model whereby the business organization was subsumed into the market. Structure was thus defined as an extension to the market. The second was through the Taylorist and management science movements, where organizations were seen as no more than vehicles for management control. In neither case was sufficient analytical sensitivity provided to appreciate the close relationship between structure and its technology.

Today, different ideas about organization arc prolific. The traditional views are still around but there are many others which have greater sophistication and which span a range of academic disciplines. They can be condensed into three major perspectives or metaphors. Scott, for example, identified these as follows. Firstly, organizations are rational systems, based upon some collective rationale such as profit maximization or growth. This perspective also embraces the two approaches already mentioned above. Secondly, organizations are natural systems; arising from the behaviourist movement of Elton Mayo this perspective views organizations as a living organism. Thirdly, organizations as open systems which are seen as processes being open to the environment.

Watson, on the other hand, identified 'waves' of organization theory. The first sees organizations as machines, portraying the view that, like machines, they are predictable. The second wave sees organizations as organisms to demonstrate that they are as complex and unpredictable as a living organism. The final wave sees organizations as processes, thus highlighting their dependence upon interactive behaviour. Others, such as Gareth Morgan, have gone further in identifying metaphors of organization (brain, machine, psychological prison, etc.) that we use to aid our understanding of them. Whichever perspective is supported, they all agree that organization structure provides some form of framework.

Mintzberg's book places considerable emphasis on structure and his definition proposes it as the summation of the ways in which a firm's labour is directed and co-ordinated into tasks. Although this definition's simplicity is appealing, it leads us to view an organization in terms of a division of labour and the co-ordination of management control to maintain that. It is an outlook typically portrayed by the firm's organization/ management chart, which identifies quite precisely who is responsible for what and to whom. This merely lists a functional relationship, which although important, reveals only part of the organization structure. Handy hints that there may be more when he talks of linking mechanisms between roles and co-ordinating structures. Although the elements of line control and co-ordination are still present, Handy extends his definition to cover the perceptual domains of an organization. This can lead to a more open definition. The concept of linkages increases our awareness of both interdependence and independence between factions; of how resource groupings can either contradict or complement other resource groupings. Linkaging is, therefore, necessary to cement the otherwise contradictory elements to prevent dispersal, or to reaffirm the complementary to prevent them becoming contradictory.

Linkaging, therefore, provides the organization with its completeness, establishes a boundary (perceptual or physical) which can be identified as being the domain of a particular organization. The idea of a boundary is an important aspect of structure since it enables us to determine how integrated the structure is with both its internal and external environments. For managers also, the boundary is useful since it enables them to identify their area of control. However, with the increasing implementation of information technology the issue has taken on greater significance. Boundaries can no longer be so easily identified. Modern technological systems directly link organizations into other organizations, thus merging in part their established boundaries. For example, a major retail outlet requires all its suppliers to link into their own stock control network. Those firms have thus become tied into their customer. In this situation it is difficult to determine where the supplier's boundary ends and the customer's begins.

Robbins proposes a traditional view of the relationship between a structure and its boundary. He determines the structure being defined by its boundary in the same way that a human skeleton defines a person. However, by equating boundary with human skeletons he has missed an important point. The body of a person is a finite concept in that it is spatially bounded within the physical domain.

On the other hand, an organizational structure, although providing a framework, is as much perceptual as physical. That is, it exists because its members perceive it to do so. To someone who does not understand the concept of an organization, the distribution of its physical resources has no significance and thus they will not see an organization. This problem is not as remote as it may appear. It is common, for example, for small business organizations to share resources such as office space, equipment and even staff, therefore possessing the same physical structure. There is no suggestion, however, that they are the same organization. Their differentiation is thus established by the perception of the actors (employees, suppliers, customers, etc.) and not the physical aspects. Organizations are not like people even though they comprise them. They are not necessarily spatially bounded; their buildings, for example, do not represent their outer edges. Indeed, some organizations have no formality about them or physical structure, such as some political or religious institutions, but they are just as real as a small business enterprise. Organizations are not bounded by a temporal framework in the same way that people are. Individuals have their historicities which influence their behaviour, but they are creatures of the here and now. Their socialization has made them believe that all there exists is the physical domain which is governed by the present. The operational levels of organizations are also bounded by time and the physical domain. However, the structure is not. It exists in the minds of its members and therefore is in the present, but it is also equally valid in the past because its existence is just as dependent upon past interaction.

For example, a firm's production process, which forms part of its structure, is physically bounded by time. It can produce only so many items within an hour or a day. This is its operational level—the dimension of doing. But the same process is time independent because how it can produce is and will be determined by decisions taken in the past, the present and the future. Structure, therefore, has to be more than a static framework, of functional and co-ordinative hierarchy, because organizations themselves are fluid, perceptual entities and as such could not be supported by a rigid framework. Robbins' model of complexity, formalization and centralization does suggest a certain fluidity in structure, but only to the extent of differentiation between particular organizations and not within the unit itself. In other words, Robbins recognizes an infinite variety of structures befitting the mode of operation, but once set they provide a rigid framework in the short term which can be changed only in the longer term. This definition would certainly not suit Watson.

Watson's ideas about an organization's structure provide a better match for a considerably more complex form of structure than so far developed. He does not see structure as a given framework but rather as a fluid, abstract entity which is the outcome of ever-changing employee interaction. Such a view can present no definitive solution to the quest for perfection, because the outcome is dependent upon so many variables.

With such a cost comes also a benefit. There is a freeing of structure from the constraints of 'conventional wisdom', by allowing greater flexibility in organization design and therefore enabling a more appropriate framework to be established for the analysis of the impact of other forces such as technology. Watson's words reflect a school of thought which considers the only reality of an organization is to be found within our minds. The structure we put on that organization is also within our minds. It will change as people's actions and perceptions change, and can never be completely controlled. Innovating forces like information technology, for example, can have the greatest impact upon an organization's structure through the minds of its participants. Structural change could occur through differing actions/perceptions of the employees, which may be beyond the control of management.

Structure must be seen to be more than a rigid framework. It may well be that some organizational structures have become increasingly flexible in the past few years as a consequence of their information technology systems. However, it would also seem likely that structures have never been as rigid as many would suggest. Some are more stable than others within a given period. Others are more responsive to certain situations such as crisis or particular market conditions. They may all have areas of rigidity within them which can subsequently cause problems. Whatever their apparent characteristics they are manifest not because of the way we organize our physical resources but rather as a consequence of the way we relate to those resources. Structure is indeed in our minds. As such any boundaries which are obvious to us are there only because we perceive them to be. If we then introduce a technology with a strong perceptual impact, such as information technology, it is not surprising that a change occurs in the way we view our organization. Such changed perception may lead to a changed structure.

The idea that organizations are perceptual maps has implications for their analysis and design. How we view them, and hence how they manifest themselves, will depend upon the particular organizational model we use. Thus in a self-determining way we align our particular organization's characteristics, as far as possible, to those found within the model which matches our own opinions. For example, if we believe along with my colleagues that the most realistic metaphor for an organization is a machine in terms of formality and controllability, then our behaviour would be governed by that belief. The organizational structure would then be affected and to a limited extent changed by such perceptions if there is not a match. Problems can occur, of course, if these perceptions are not fully disseminated throughout the organization. The models of organization we have, therefore, are themselves affecting the environment which they are attempting to analyse. From this aspect alone it is worth while determining what these models are. However, we need to also consider them in terms of their suitability for the impact analysis of information technology.

The mechanistic view of organization is the first wave of theory, which comprises the metaphor of organization as a machine. Like a machine, its characteristics are determinable and controllable. The degree of its formality is not considered because all actions and behaviour within it are considered to be purposeful and co-ordinated. In other words, organizations are rational processes. Therefore the underlying assumption is one of an organization as a formalization of a need to meet certain objectives. Such objectives are seen as rational in that they are based upon an obvious range of criteria suitable for the type of organization. Thus a business organization's objectives could be to maximize profits, to grow or to dominate a particular market or industry.

The emphasis is on goal attainment and its management. The profound question presented by this metaphor is, why are some managements better at achieving their objectives than others? This metaphor evolved from the economic model in which organizations are perceived to be unitary entities pursuing the same collective objective, controlled and driven by market forces. As such, organizations do not have any analytical value other than as a unit of the market. From this, however, four softer perspectives developed, each a response to the demand of business managements at the time for better understanding.

The first is Taylor's scientific management. The second is administrative principles proposed by people such as Henri Fayol. The third is Weber's theory of bureaucracy, and lastly Simon's discussion on administrative behaviour. There are many books which cover these areas quite adequately. Apart from an introduction below, these will not be dealt with in detail. The emphasis will be placed on examining their approaches to technology.

The founding father of the scientific movement is claimed to be Frederick Taylor and subsequently developed by others such as Lillian Gilbreth. Their perspective is an extension of the economic model by recognizing that organizations are not determined solely by market forces but can be molded by management activity. They prescribed a methodology for action through a scientific analysis of tasks in a firm so that formal procedures could be established for optimum efficiency. The approach, in short, is prescriptive in that it presents patterns for management behaviour. Although lacking in fundamental academic support the traditions of scientific management are still reflected in many of our management training programmes.

The 'modern' view is more developed in its recognition of greater uncertainty but nevertheless still portrays a controllable environment. The elements of that environment are also controllable, Thus the notion of technology is coloured by the certainty of its predictability. Technology in all its forms is a management tool. The original exponents of scientific management thought this, as do their followers. There is no relationship between a structure and its technology because neither is seen as a social process but rather as building blocks for management use. Thus the impact of innovations such as information technology is not seen to affect the organizational structure as such, but rather the relationship between management and workers: any impact is regarded as an input to be controlled.

Innovation, therefore, changes only the way in which management operates (although this might have an indirect effect upon the organization itself). Impact assessment of information technology is in terms of functional analysis or efficiency criteria (how good or bad its contribution is to management objectives), the assumption being that the technology will always fit into existing organizational structures with the appropriate implementation strategy. The emphasis, therefore, is on performance measures and the ability of information technology to meet them. There is a range of literature which explores the scientific management viewpoint of information technology. Its presentation is prescriptive and consultative.

The remaining three perspectives within this metaphor are dealt with under the one heading. They are the models initiated by Fayol, Weber and Simon. Their collation is not because the themes they support are necessarily in agreement, although they do cover broadly the same principles, but rather because their implications for the analysis of technology are similar. The major difference between these and the previous approaches is that scientific management sought to establish the organization as a management phenomenon whereas Fayol, Weber and Simon sought to establish the organization as an administrative process.

The immediate implication of this is that, as an administrative process, the organization is less controllable and less predictable. It is no longer a tool but a set of administrative interactions. The objective of this group, therefore, was to identify such interactions and then to determine their appropriate control. Fayol was perhaps the first to recognize the importance of the administrative process in understanding organization. However, his work was not translated until the late 1940s and thus not widely known.

A sociologist, Max Weber, was also developing an ideological set of administrative principles. He identified bureaucracy as being the ideal form of organization. The formal and impersonal structural characteristics allowed for the most appropriate administrative processes and for an efficient achievement of objectives coupled with a certain humanity. Although advances were being made in other areas, it was not until the late 1950s, with the appearance of Herbert Simon's ideas, that advances in this area were made. He sought to portray a more open administrative process in which the actors are not machine-like in their rationality but more human in pursuing their own interests and in many ways ignorant of their total environment. He saw their rationality bounded by the complexity of the environment and thus their decision-making was not perfect or indeed predictable. Simon, along with others such as Cyert and March, perhaps provided the link between this metaphor and the second wave. They viewed people as being less predictable than did their forebears, but still nevertheless determined the organization itself to be of machine-like stature.

Perhaps by default, technology is, therefore, more integrated into the administrative mechanisms of the organization. There is concern about technological fit, thus the approach is directed away from one of expert handling to one of greater integration. This is particularly evident in this view's handling of information technology. The literature which reflects it concentrates upon the user end: it is here that a controllable interface exists between the administrative process and the machine. A classic example of this view is to be found in a book by Whisler, although it is becoming dated. In the 1980s, with the increasing power of computer technology, many other books found their way onto the market. They all sought to merge the computer with the work processes of the organization rather than to allow it to dominate them, but stopped short of seeing it as a social process.

Peter Blau determined that it is irrational to view an organization as rational in the way that the machine metaphor does because it does not take account of the non-rational behaviour of people. Such a perspective summarizes the natural or organismic metaphor, in that organizations are seen as complex, living entities which do not have machine-like qualities. They are no longer reified, cohesive units which act in harmony and with total rationality towards a common set of goals. In the same way that a living organism is a collection of competing and interacting forces, some living and some not, so too the organization comprises individuals and social forces which compete with and contradict each other.

The consequence is that the organization cannot be so easily prescribed for management action, being at best a rather fuzzy area for common agreement. Technology, therefore, as an element of organization, cannot be so predictable in terms of a resource. Neither is there agreement on how to model the metaphor. With some justification it is claimed that Elton Mayo provided a foundation with his Hawthorne experiments. As social psychologists, their contribution was in recognizing the importance of behaviour in organizational design. Their work initiated the behaviourist school for the explanation of firms.

The offshoots are many and are still very much in vogue today. Since Weber's work the sociologists have also been major contributors to this metaphor, particularly through the work of Selznick and Parsons. Rather than placing the emphasis upon the people element of an organization as the behaviourists did, these and other theorists who followed were interested in the complete entity and how it worked. In true functionalist tradition they identified various component parts and studied interaction between them. Selznick highlighted the relationship between these and the organization's employees, whilst Parsons developed a dynamic model in which people were an integrated part. The technological tradition which grew from this metaphorical approach is less prescriptive and more analytical than that of the machine metaphor.

The earlier ideas are typically represented by the works of Gouldner or Wedderburn and Crompton. Theirs is mainly an examination of production technology and its relationship with the workforce. The structure of an organization was a consequence of the way its workforce produced, in particular of the relationship existing between workforce and technology. However, a more formalized development of this took place in the late 1950s and early 1960s which was influenced in part by Elton Mayo and also by considerable empirical research. Although not labelled until much later, the approach became known as contingency theory. In contrast to the classical approach (whether the machine or natural metaphor) which sought to achieve a universally best structure for a business organization, the contingency theory proposes that there is no one best solution.

Different situations demand different organizational structures, which are governed by forces of change known as contingencies. Thus the prevailing contingent would shape the corresponding organizational structure. For Woodward, after extensive research of over a hundred firms in Essex, the most important contingent is technology. If, for instance, a firm has a mass production technology, then its structure would develop in terms of the other contingents, such as size and culture, which would best suit that. So mass production technology, for example, by its very nature determines that firms generally be large with formal cultures. Quite apparently, therefore, technology is seen by Woodward as a determinant of organization. Although others, such as Pugh and the Aston Group, do not agree with her upon the extent of the power of technology to determine structure, there is a general consensus on the nature of technology itself. It is no longer a resource as such, but as much an element of organizations as structure, people and their culture.

Information technology is perhaps not addressed as positively as it is in the previous metaphor. This is because there is no formal distinction made between general technology and information technology. Both are social processes and therefore to be treated as such. That is not to say there are not writers on the subject. Miles *et al.*, Anderson and Mumford and Zuboff are typical of the works produced. Information technology is analysed in terms of its ability to integrate into society or business. In general, the conclusions seem to be doom-laden, predicting dire consequences if we do not get it right.

ORGANIZATIONS AS PROCESSES

This metaphor describes the organization as a complex conglomerate of interaction which does not necessarily produce a clearly identifiable form. An organization exists because people are told it does by management teams, corporate identity and so on; although, in reality, apart from resource allocation, members/employees act very much for themselves as individuals or within groups, occasionally forming alliances to get things done. It is the process of doing (production, administration, etc.) which is the major input to organization structure, so that the organization is a series of different or interlocking processes. Its structure is shaped by those processes because it is the arena in which they are actioned. As with the other two waves there are disagreements, in particular over the identity of the process. Some put forward the decision process as a dynamic which determines the organizational structure. Others view the organization as a political arena in which structural adjustments are made through political mechanisms such as ownership of power. Yet others, such as Johnson *et al.*, regard these processes in terms of their relationships with one another and how open they are to external influence. Contingency theorists Lawrence and Lorsch, on the other hand, determined a particular relationship between the organization and its environment as being the important process, whilst Weick highlighted the processes between the individual and their social formation.

In general, organizations are no longer seen as hierarchical and solid (albeit at times fuzzy) frameworks. Structure is considered not to be as important as the processes themselves because it is a transient thing, created and remolded by the whim of changing interactions. Watson described this organization as being formed in the minds of the employees through their perception of its interactions. The process or open systems metaphor, therefore, shifts the emphasis of analysis from the design of the organization to the functioning of its elements. It allows these elements (e.g. technology, politics, decisions) a far greater impact than the previous two metaphors. For technology in particular the approach is significant. In the machine metaphor, technology is not part of the organization, whilst in the organismic metaphor technology is part of an organization's social process and a determinant of structure. In the process metaphor, technology can be a process in its own right, determining the perceptions of individuals and affecting their behaviour. Its ability to affect the characteristics of an organization are thus considerably increased because the mechanisms involved (i.e. employee perception) form the essence of an organization. These ideas have been most prevalent in the analysis of information technology. The relationship between the behaviour of people and the technology they use is portrayed by the socio-technical systems theory. This applies a systems methodology to the analysis of information technology and how it affects the way we organize. Its roots can be traced back to Mayo and his Hawthorne experiments in terms of the paradigm's behavioural aspirations. It was Mayo who first formally stated the link between our behaviour and organizational design. But It was Trist and Bamforth who galvanized those ideas into understanding the impact of technological innovation.

With the growth of computer technology as the dominant innovative technology it was, therefore, not surprising that Trist and Bamforth's methodology was quickly taken up by others to analyse its impact. Burns and Stalker produced an impressive model based upon empirical research describing a close behavioural relationship between our technology and the way we organized. If the structure of the firm did not suit the technology employed then pathological responses evolved on the part of management.

SEEKING A SOLUTION

Just as firms are not merely a collection of resources, human or otherwise, nor are they merely a collection of processes. As with all social entities, they are a combination of physical and perceptual: but it is how the relationship between the two is understood which is important. Quite obviously many organizations do have buildings which figure strongly in the image they project but also quite obviously the influence of the organization does not end at a brick wall. They do comprise physical beings constrained by their physical environment but beyond such environments they have resources which can be both physical (machinery, etc.) and perceptual (knowledge). Any complete model of organization must accommodate both domains. Organizations, however, must be more than the summation of individuals, resources and perceptions within them. Unfortunately the metaphors discussed describe no more than this. Yet organizations tend to develop some sense of being in their own right. This is not in terms of a conscious, spatial positioning, as any individual would have, but is rather a consequence of history.

Continuity of an organization, for example, cannot be solely explained as the perception of individuals or the particular allocation of resourcing. There is a logic within it which outlives any temporary input an individual may care to make. It is indeed a process, but one which is at the same time both independent and dependent. For example, previous decisions made by management can constrain and develop the organization's structure in future years. Both the physical and perceptual aspects of the decision described in Case Study 4.2 are as real as each other. One could be seen in the production line whilst the other, although not seen, is ingrained within the management culture. Together they form ail inheritance passed onto subsequent management which constrains their action. It is in this sense that an organization can be said to be existing independently. Decisions and actions are taken all the time which can then exist beyond their initiators and add to a bank of knowledge within the firm. To a certain extent we are referring to the organizational culture, but culture's form relates only to the rules for action and does not express the logic of the actions themselves, as does structure. Structure can thus be determined by neither domain alone. More probably, it arises as a consequence of a relationship between the two domains continually interacting with one another through a historical process which in turn feeds the logic of the organization. In the same vein, information technology (or technology in general) cannot be treated as either a physical or perceptual phenomenon.

The way in which each of the three metaphors provides analytical tools for the assessment of its impact restricts our being able to see the whole framework. Information technology does have a strong physical impact: it can, for example, turn an inefficient firm into an efficient one. The criteria used to assess such a change are based in the physical domain in that there can be more information output in terms of management reports or invoices billed and so on. It can also change user behaviour, as we see in socio-technical systems, so that employee perceptions of their tasks or indeed their firm change. In many models the two domains sit either separately or uncomfortably side by side.

However, it is not so much the consideration of the individual domains that is important (although obviously for line managers it cannot be ignored), it is the relationship between them which must be analysed and the subsequent effects such interaction has upon organization design.

4

Network Communications

This chapter briefly indicates the fundamental problems of data communications, and gives an overview of the broad approaches which have been taken towards them. A computer network is intended to connect together a wide range of information technology equipment, which varies in the design and operation of the equipment itself, in the information types it handles, and in the internal processing which it undertakes. In order to be able to communicate successfully, these various systems must have a common 'language' for the exchange of information, while retaining their local independence.

As well as an agreed form for communication the network units must also agree on the *process* of communicating—the rules which govern the procedures for the exchange of information and the co-ordination of action between participants. In daily communication we use a language to express our ideas and intentions, and the voice as a means of transmitting this information to other people.

To ensure that the communication is successful, we must converse in an agreed language which the hearer is able to understand, and we must be able to respond to messages asking for clarification, repetition, and so on. In any conversation, there are well-understood rules which govern the process of communication—taking turns, allowing others a chance to speak, indicating that one has finished speaking, waiting until another has finished before speaking oneself, and so on. These signals are often given implicitly, through signs such as gestures or tone of voice.

The data communication process has to be much more structured and organized in style, spelled out in every detail, since these tacit factors are missing from a machine-based process. The rules for communication must be well defined and standardized; there is little room for 'working out' what a participant in the exchange really meant to say. This process underlies the development of sophisticated and 'user-friendly' applications which depend on network communication, even though this may not be immediately apparent.

A goal of information networking is to allow users to work in this medium as naturally as possible, finding the least obtrusive fit with the natural work environment. A dialogue which is mediated by computer communication places certain structural constraints on the process due to these underlying factors; the task of design is to find ways of incorporating the equivalent of the contextual factors which inform human communication while working within these constraints.

A basic model of the communication process identifies the entities involved, and their respective roles. There are three main elements:

— a sender, which originates the message, and is responsible for representing the content of the message in an agreed format;

— a channel, which carries the message from sender to recipient through some physical medium;

— a recipient, which receives the message, and is responsible for interpreting the format in order to extract the information content.

The communication is not simply one way, and the roles will at times be reversed: the recipient may wish to send a reply to the original message.

In network communications explicit signals and format rules are vital to the success of the communications process. For a computing machine to manage this role effectively, rules governing these issues must be highly detailed and agreed in advance, and encapsulated in software programs. Data and communications software must be able to deal with management of the exchange process, not only by sending and receiving messages for transmission but also by encoding and decoding between the internal format used by the computer and the format used for external communication. It is also necessary to monitor the quality of the exchange and to co-ordinate activity between participants at each end of the process for longer data exchanges. This is problematic because the channel which links the participants will have characteristics of its own which may affect the communication process.

The sender and recipient exchange the encoded message as a physical signal transmitted in some way through a common channel. The environment of this channel can potentially interfere with and distort the signals in the process, resulting in the loss of some information content and delivery of a corrupted message. This kind of interference is known as noise—the general effect of corruption and garbling of the signal which occurs after it has been transmitted, and before it is received. For example, noise may result in the appearance of unreadable characters on a computer screen in the midst of a normal text message, as the receiving system attempts to interpret corrupted signalling codes.

Although the use of more reliable technology for the transmission medium has reduced the problem of noise in recent years, the rules which govern the process of communication must still be capable of detecting and recovering from the effects of noise by returning a message to its original form. This requires the communications software to have some means of matching the two versions of the message—that sent and that received—and entails the addition of control information to the actual data content by one means or another. Thus the exchange will consist of more than the simple data content of the message.

Techniques for dealing with the effects of noise are concerned to preserve the quality of the message by ensuring that the integrity of the signs used to represent the information content have not been compromised. The communication process must also therefore be concerned with co-ordinating the system of codes which is used to express the semantic qualities of the data exchange—what might be loosely called the 'meaning' of the message; with the physical representation of the chosen coding system as transmittable signals; and with any control information which binds different elements of the message together.

There are various different coding systems for the task of mapping information generated by user applications into the binary codes used by the computer. For text, the ASCII (American Standard Character Set for Information Interchange) is widely used both within a computer and for data interchange purposes; however, completely different character sets are used in some circumstances, for instance the EBCDIC character set which dominates the IBM mainframe world.

There are several different representation formats for graphics, which may be either bit patterns or geometric coordinates, and for other forms such as video signals and multimedia information. For meaningful information to be exchanged there must be agreement between the end systems on the method by which the message is represented for transmission, even though this may not affect the actual exchange of data symbols through the channel. Since there is little standardization in the internal processes of computer equipment itself, the actual physical signals which the end systems generate must also be standardized for inter-operability, and may need translation between different physical forms in order to make use of different communication channels.

The additional control information which is appended to the user data content carries information used in processing the message, and must also conform to some agreed system. A simple text message, for example, may contain an, overhead of information which is used to indicate boundaries between characters or chunks of text; this will appear as binary digits apparently identical to the data content unless there is some common method of 'reading' the stream of symbols.

A multimedia message which contains both sound and video elements requires control information to synchronize timing of the audio output with the screen display, which must be interpreted correctly.

There is a need to synchronize the flow of information between the two end systems, so that signals which will conflict with each other are not generated simultaneously, and so that the receiver is ready and capable of processing the incoming signals at the rate which they are sent—controlling the 'turn taking'.

Communication can take place in one of two alternative patterns, and in each of these synchronization is achieved in different ways. Asynchronous communication might be characterized as 'on demand' use of the communications channel. All network users have equal access to the channel, and use it to send messages at random intervals, characterized by short bursts of activity with quiet periods of varying length in between. The receiver waits passively once the connection is made, and is activated by the receipt of some message. A typical example of this type of activity would result from a user seated at a terminal screen, alternating interaction with a remote computer with periods of planning and thinking.

Synchronous communication depends on a fixed cycle, in which each user, and both sender and receiver, have access to the channel at defined time intervals for a fixed period. A typical use for this approach would be for large data file transfers in situations where the transfer is being managed completely by the computer systems as a background process, with no human intervention, or for the synchronization of composite sound and video signals in videoconferencing systems. This synchronicity characteristic delineates the time/response dimension of the process, defining the appropriate activities in the end systems to control the process; there is also a characteristic of the communication channel which will affect the process.

Communication through a transmission channel can occur in one of three different modes determining the allowed direction of, and activity in, the transmission. Each of these requires a different level of sophistication in control of the communication process:

— in simplex mode, the communication is in one direction only;

— in half-duplex mode, the communication can be bi-directional, but at alternate times only;

— in full-duplex mode, the communication is bi-directional, and both end systems may transmit simultaneously.

The term *channel* is normally used to denote the more abstract concept of a logical channel rather than the actual physical media. One physical link may potentially offer several logical communication channels, which can be thought of as separate entities.

Since a network is a medium which is shared by many users, management of the communication process is a more complex affair than is suggested by the simplified one-to-one model. As well as agreeing on the terms by which the exchange will be conducted, the communication program must be able to supervise and regulate the dynamic elements of the process, making necessary adjustments as the exchange develops and operating conditions fluctuate. The communications program must be able to:

— establish and maintain a connection across the communications channel between the sender and recipient, agree the terms on which the exchange is to be conducted, and terminate the connection-once the transaction is completed;

— regulate the flow of information between the two participants to prevent overloading of data by the recipient, if it is unable to process it quickly enough, and a consequent possible loss of information;

— control the quality of information received by checking for the presence of errors and taking corrective action as necessary, perhaps by requesting a re-transmission of corrupted information.

The term bandwidth is an indication of the information capacity of an individual element in the process: the higher the bandwidth of the channel, for example, the higher is its information carrying capacity. The overall communication process (including the end systems) can only utilize the information-carrying capacity of the element with the least available bandwidth in any particular situation; either the transmitter, the receiver, or the channel will have a more limited bandwidth and will define the overall information exchange rate. In many situations, the bandwidth of the communication channel will be the limiting factor.

The capacity of a channel is normally expressed as the number of distinct symbols per second which can be passed along it. This maximum *data transfer rate* is usually given as a figure measured in bits per second, since the number of bits which make up a useful 'unit' of information will differ according to the information type—between characters of text and scanned images in bit-map form, for instance. In this way, a channel which is described as having a particular data transfer rate can be matched to different information transfer processes through a common comparable measure.

In some circumstances, particularly in modem communications, the term *baud rate* is popularly used as an equivalent to this measure of bits per second; although this is not a strictly accurate use of the term, it can normally be taken to mean the same thing. Transmission channels can also be characterized by the method of signalling which is used. In *baseband* signalling the capacity of the channel is monopolised by a single message for the duration of the transmission, typically by varying the voltage along an electrical cable in a pre-determined pattern.

Broadband signalling enables a physical medium to be shared by more than one transmission by varying the frequency of the signals to ensure separation of one from the other—as a radio can distinguish different frequency transmissions. Broadband offers a higher bandwidth, and is therefore more associated with information networking applications which require higher capacities, such as multimedia. A goal of advanced network technology is to support a flexible, use of bandwidth among multiple users according to fluctuating demand, changing the allocation dynamically according to the transmission needs of the moment.

A communication channel is a logical concept that can be implemented on a variety of physical media, each of which has its own particular characteristics, such as bandwidth. The choice of which to adopt depends on the purposes of the network and the kind of applications it must support, the predicted traffic and data rates together with required response times, and a cost/benefit calculation on the relative importance between these factors. The most widely used physical transmission media are mentioned here.

1. The *twisted pair* is the simplest form of transmission cable, two simple electrical cables carrying small voltage signals. This is a very cheap method of connecting individual computer devices to a network, and is easy to install, but is not suitable for carrying traffic from many devices due to the limited bandwidth which it possesses, nor for applications which require more than a 1 Megabit per second (Mbps) data rate.

2. *Co-axial cable* uses a more substantial copper cable to offer a higher bandwidth suitable for multiple access from a limited number of nodes on a local network; and for the transmission of information forms which

require a higher throughput of data, such as video signals, at data rates of up to 10 Mbps. This higher capacity is bought, at the expense of a higher material cost and a more complex installation process.

3. *Optical fibre cable* provides a means of transcending the physical limits of electrical cable, by conveying signals on a fluctuating light beam enclosed within a very fine glass fibre. Since light waves have a much higher potential bandwidth than electrical waves, data rates up to and beyond 100 Mbps are possible, as well as providing a lower susceptibility to noisy or sensitive environments.

   A single glass fibre, smaller in dimension than a human hair, is provided for each signal, and an installed optical cable may consist of several hundred fibres bundled together, providing a high throughput for existing services and spare capacity for future growth. While optical fibre provides a means of building very high bandwidth networks which can support sophisticated multimedia services, it is expensive and more difficult to install, requiring special interface equipment between cable and computer.

4. Microwave transmission offers a non-terrestrial alternative to a physical point-to-point link. Data is conveyed on radio waves through free space, and is normally used in conjunction with geostationary satellites. The data is transmitted from a ground station, called an uplink, to an orbiting satellite which is in direct line-of-sight, and the signal is bounced back to a receiving station (the downlink) at some different geographical ground location. These re-transmissions can be broadcast over a wide area for receiving by many destinations simultaneously, or be highly focused onto a single site.

Satellite relay is commonly used to leap across long distances, such as in establishing connections between the United Kingdom and North America or the Far East, or where the laying of a physical cable would be costly or impossible across difficult geographic terrain. Microwave transmission may also be used on a ground-to-ground basis, between stations situated on high ground within line of sight of each other.

5. Network communications have also been achieved by the use of infra-red and broadcast radio signals; there is a growing interest in the use of such 'wireless' communications although few actual installations as yet. Some use is made of radio data broadcasting at a national level.

Essentially, a protocol is one attempt to address the basic problems of data communications which are relevant to networking within a particular arena. Since there is no universally applicable solution to these problems which will be effective in all situations, a range of protocols have arisen which have proved effective in specialized areas within the current feasible limits of technology. Since the development of communication protocols has been carried out within the context of perceived practical problems, there is a tendency for the available offerings to be predicated on the use of particular types and make of equipment.

Computer manufacturers have devised their own proprietary protocol suites intended to interconnect only their own Computer makes; and more generally applicable protocols have emerged for broader categories of computer, such as for local networks of micro-computers. Although a protocol is a logical specification rather than a particular implementation in software, the protocol is likely to make assumptions about available levels of functionality and processing capabilities.

As both computing technology and information applications have led to more complicated and sophisticated systems, so the communications process between systems has also developed a parallel level of complexity. The complexity of modern networking has led to the use of a layered approach to protocol specification. A l*ayered protocol* aims to analyse the overall communications process into well-defined and semi-autonomous functional modules, each of which provides a specialized service in the overall scheme and works in conjunction with the other modules.

Network communications can then be split into constituent activities, and these may be implemented on different parts of the system in different ways, not necessarily all together on the same piece of equipment. Any particular layer may potentially contain alternative specifications for reaching the same goals, each of which is more appropriate for a particular environment or system arrangement.

As long as the module provides the appropriate service to its co-operating modules in the process, the way in which it achieves this need not concern the other elements involved. This kind of arrangement provides a greater flexibility in interconnecting different types of system which conform to the same layered framework. There is not, unfortunately, any universal or even dominant agreement on one scheme for dividing logical functions up into different layers.

The growing need for the capability of interconnecting computer systems and networks whatever their local characteristics has led to several initiatives aiming to develop a degree of standardization between the major alternatives, and to encourage the conformity of new products to these standards. These initiatives aim to develop a framework within which the most widely accepted and established 'industry standard' protocols can fit as alternative options. At the present time networking protocols fall into two main groups:

— those emanating from or supported by national and international standards making bodies, which are more 'open' in nature with published specifications;

— those emerging as proprietary standards from major computer manufacturers, which are 'closed' by virtue of their confidential specification and non-participative development.

A set of protocols will deal with aspects which are more closely related to the physical aspects of data and network communications and those which are more related to the information transfer aspects of user activity. At the lower layers, the data communications aspects can be seen as failing into three main areas: the physical connection, basic data management, and routing through the network.

The *physical level* is concerned with producing, receiving and monitoring the physical signals which are actually transmitted between systems, and with the standardization of methods for representing data in this form. A well-known example of this is the RS-232C standard, which defines the electrical interface on equipment as a multi-pin connection and assigns a particular function to each pin. The *data link level* is concerned with error control and recovery, and with flow control. In order to achieve this, most protocols encapsulate the user data in frames by dividing the stream of data into units of a pre-defined size and adding control information for use by the receiving system.

Since the network connection will be conveying data frames from other network users, the frames also contain header information ensuring delivery to the correct destination. Special frames may also be used to send only control information, for example to establish and terminate links with a remote computer. The frames produced by this layer are passed down to the physical layer for transmission. Error control is important at this level, since noise on the channel may result in the loss or corruption of frames; one purpose of splitting the whole message up into data frames is to retain control of the transmission as it develops, and take any remedial action necessary. Error control takes a number of simpler or more sophisticated forms, some of which require feedback from the receiver, for example:

— echo checking reflects characters received back to the sender for display on the user's screen, so that any corruption can be noticed and re-transmitted;

— acknowledgement schemes require the receiver to send an acknowledgement token back to the sender for each frame, before the next is transmitted;

— check digits can be added to the data frame by the sender, based on a computation carried out on the user data itself, and which the receiver can also use to check comparability.

Flow control is concerned to ensure that the data is not sent faster than it can be received; this function can make use of some of these devices, for instance acknowledgement schemes, or add features of its own to the exchange process. The network level is concerned with the management and control of routing through the network. The extent to which this is relevant will depend on the type of network in use and the mode in which it is operating. There are two broad modes within which a network can operate, providing two types of service:

— *connectionless mode*, in which the data is dispatched by the sender with the appropriate destination address, but no direct connection is made between them;

— *connection-oriented mode,* in which the two end systems behave as though directly connected by a physical medium and work in co-operation with each other.

A network may offer both these types of service as alternatives, but cannot normally support mixing between the two types. The network layer will typically organize the user data into packets, splitting up a long message into several units in this way, and adding source and destination information to each packet to control its path through the network. The user data is then made transparent to the network itself, which is only concerned with the 'external' address information. Different packets which constitute parts of the same message are then treated as independent units, and may travel through the network at different speeds and by different routes.

The receiving system takes delivery of the packets and reconstitutes the message in its original format using the control information added by the sender. An X.25 network is an example of this arrangement. The network layer passes the packets down to the data link layer for the addition of error and flow control information, once it has completed its own responsibilities. In this way, user data is passed between layers in both sender and receiver, with only one actual physical network connection between them. In wider area networks, these three layers are also contained within the intermediate stages internal to the network, as well as in the end systems.

The specific protocols which implement these broad functions within an individual context will depend on the particular elements of the system which is in use, and the equipment available to it. A range of protocols are implemented either as software in communications packages, or as hardware built into data communications equipment. Some have achieved a greater popularity and therefore a *de facto* standardization over time.

In order for the communication process to be successful, both systems which intend to exchange data must be capable of running the same protocol, and therefore require communications packages or hardware which are compatible with each other; larger systems may offer a range of communication alternatives which can sense the method used by a caller and select the appropriate option. The types of device which have a role to play in the entire networking process can be placed into two categories:

1. Data terminating equipment (DTE) describes the devices which originate, or provide the final destination for, a transmitted message; either that operated by an end-user, or a computer system working autonomously. Typical examples of DTE devices would be a desktop microcomputer, a mainframe computer system, a visual display unit terminal, a printer, or a facsimile machine.
2. Data communicating equipment (DCE) describes the devices which are used to support onwards communication of a message received from some DTE device type—acting as 'steps in the chain' rather than as end-controllers of the process. This may be a device attached to the end-user's system, or some intermediate step within the network itself.

The data communicating equipment acts as a common interface for unlike data terminating equipment, evening out the differences through the common use of a standard protocol. In this way, dissimilar types of information technology equipment can be used for information networking without requiring an end user to be aware of the physical characteristics of the receiving system; the

More widely used and open the standard protocol which is used, the wider range of equipment which can interface in this way. The kind of equipment which falls into this category fulfils specialized roles in the communications process: some of these are integral to the internal functioning of the network element itself while others are associated with user end systems. Some of the more commonly found types are described here, as indicative of the range.

The multiplexor is a device for concentrating a number of terminal devices onto a higher bandwidth line, to make the most effective use of this capacity and to remove the need for installing many duplicate lines (one for each device) in parallel with each other. This arrangement would typically be used to connect several terminals situated near each other to a central computer which is located at some distance.

The multiplexor is responsible for apportioning the line on an equitable basis between all the terminals connected. There are two main methods of multiplexing:

— time-division multiplexing, in which each terminal is allotted the full capacity of the channel for a fixed period of time, in a rotating sequence;

— frequency division multiplexing, in which the full channel capacity is divided between users by allowing simultaneous transmissions on different frequencies.

The most appropriate form to use depends on the applications which are using the system; commonly asynchronous enquiry-type applications, where activity is in unpredictable short bursts, use a time-division form of multiplexing. A multiplexor must be installed at the receiving end, to separate out the different terminal signals for processing.

A modem is another communicating device which allows one kind of DTE equipment, typically a personal computer, to establish a temporary connection with another remote computer system by using the normal telephone line. Since the telephone system was originally designed solely for voice traffic, which is analogue in nature, some conversion process must be used to translate digital computer data into a form suitable for analogue transmission. Digital signals are in a binary form, having two states—on and off—which can be represented as changes in voltage signals on a cable.

Since the normal telephone line is designed for transmission of sound waves, these binary signals must be transformed into an audible tone by the modem. This process is known as modulation; a modem (modulator—demodulator) must be placed at both ends of the telephone link, acting as the interface between the end systems and the line, encoding and decoding the digital data signals. A series of standards recommendations have been produced by the CCITT (Comite Consultatif Internationale de Telegraphie et Telephonic), a Geneva-based international organization concerned with issues in telecommunications development, for the use of modems.

The cost of modem technology falls steadily, faster transmission speeds are achieved at a higher expense due not only to the price of equipment but also to the additional communications processing which is necessary at higher speeds. Higher transmission speeds are achieved by a panoply of special techniques which require more sophisticated error checking capabilities to counter the increased influence of noise. While the CCITT recommendations are standard within Europe, the existence of a separate set of standards in North America, developed by the Bell Communications Corporation complicates the international situation. The most common of these are the Bell 203 (1200 bps) and Bell 212 (2400 bps) standards; although working at the same speeds they do not have an exact correspondence to V-series standards and are not compatible. A final example of data communicating equipment is the use of an independent computer processor to handle the communications loading of a large computer system. This would typically be used where a mainframe computer is accessed by a large number of remote callers; for example, a system which makes an online bibliographic database available to users on a global basis through the use of modems over a telecommunications network.

A smaller computer—such as a minicomputer—is dedicated to the task of dealing with the network communications, so that the mainframe does not become overloaded by this task, and is free to concentrate on database activity. The front end processor handles the external contact, passing queries back to the database machine and forwarding results to the remote caller. The remote caller is, of course, not aware of the separation of functions.

5

Types of Computer Networks

Computer networks can be categorized along several dimensions and by differing criteria; however, there is no single set of exclusive categories into which all types can be fitted, and networks which are similar in some ways will display contrasting characteristics in others. A network consists essentially of two kinds of elements:

— the network nodes which are the actual computing end systems, for example larger computer systems, personal workstations, terminals etc;

— the connections between these along which data transmissions travel.

Network nodes can have a greater or lesser degree of autonomy in local processing power and ability to control the communication process. The connections can be implemented in various media, but in some way serve to switch data flows between these network nodes, to pass information from a source to a destination in the most appropriate way. As a first stage, networks can usefully be categorized by the type of switching which is used.

There are three basic types of switching:

— circuit switching,

— message switching;

— packet switching.

Circuit switching occurs when a physical link is made between the two network nodes for the duration of a session, along which the data can flow under the control of the end systems. The connection must be set up before the information exchange can begin, and released once the session is completed; in the interim, the circuit is only available to the two participants even though the channel may have spare capacity which is unused.

Message switching does not establish a physical connection, but relies on the network to deliver a message successfully once sent. The network is used as an intermediary: the source end system delivers the message to the network and then has no further involvement; the network will carry the message to its destination as a discrete process. The source end system is not aware of the details of this process, and does not work interactively with the destination end system. The network may use a broadcast technique to convey the message; or may route it through a series of intermediate staging posts, each of which receives the message, stores it, and forwards it on to the next step when possible.

Packet switching techniques take a more structured approach, dividing an individual message into separate 'packets', each of which can travel independently through the network. The network is responsible for the safe delivery of these packets, creating them from the message dispatched from the source end system at the point of entry to the network, and re-assembling them into the original message at the point of exit for the destination end system. Since the network is dealing with smaller standard size packets in a predetermined way, a faster transmission rate can be achieved. The network is able to make its own decisions on routing, and can change these dynamically as traffic conditions change, with no apparent difference to the end user.

A second characteristic of network types concerns the geographical extent of coverage, and the size in terms of the total number of network nodes which can be feasibly connected. A general classification is to describe networks as either:

— local area networks, which are limited to a single site or building, interconnecting nodes within a single organization;

— wide area networks, which are not geographically limited in scope, and are capable of national- and global-level interconnections.

This distinction arises from the very different technologies from which each of these approaches have grown; however, these categories are beginning to break down, as local area networks become more powerful and can themselves be interlinked to form larger entities. An intermediate category is now emerging, which can potentially provide a link between the first two:

— metropolitan area networks, which exploit the new transmission media such as fibre optic cable, to build city-wide capabilities.

Wide area networks can be usefully seen in two groups, distinguishing public and private systems:

— public telecommunications networks are international in scope, and accessible as a publicly available service;

— private data networks may also be on a national or international scale, but are intended for a distinct user group and not for general public access, although they are likely to make use of services offered by public telecommunications operators.

Each of these network types uses networking technologies which are most appropriate for their purposes.

These may be quite unlike each other, employing different techniques, principles and protocols which are not easily compatible. Stemming from these different technologies, there are consequent differences in maximum data transmission rates, number of possible network connections, response times and overloading factors etc.

Network control

The degree of control which is placed within the network, and the location of this control also arises from these differences in approach. This may be characterized along a continuum, which offers at the extremes:

— a centralized network, with a single main switch to which all nodes are connected, and through which they communicate with each other;

— a decentralised peer-to-peer network, in which each node possesses the same status as any other, and can communicate with any other of its peers on an equal basis.

For large-and small-scale networks, there are various compromise points along this continuum where they can be placed; an inter-network can also be constructed using various different topological arrangements which are interconnected at specific gateways-links from one type to the other type.

Terminal networks

Terminal networks are perhaps the simplest form of computer network, consisting of a number of relatively unintelligent terminals, each of which is linked to the central computer system and not directly to other terminals. These two elements work in a masterslave relationship to each other, in that the central system has much more extensive control of the process than the terminal, even though this may in fact be a more powerful machine, such as a personal computer emulating a terminal. In such centralized systems, the connections between terminals and central computer are arranged in a star topology, with communications routed through the central switch; if this should fail the main communication channel is cut off.

Terminal networks are very commonly used in large organizations that wish to pursue a centralized information policy, holding data and information systems at a single main point and providing widespread access to this. There may be a high level of communication requirements for this arrangement, however, where speed of response is important; for example a lending desk terminal in a branch public library may be required to- transmit loan information to a central database and check appropriate records in a very few seconds.

Micro-mainframe connections

The growth in use of desktop and personal computers has had a significant influence on the development of centralized systems, swaying the balance of control more towards the end user. This has led to attempts at creating a greater integration and cohesion between information systems at an organisational level, linking the departmental/office information into the corporate database level.

Terminal emulation packages allow the end user to utilize a familiar desktop PC as a central terminal without the need to switch equipment, and increasingly to use the computing power of the PC to improve screen presentation rather than simply emulating a dumb terminal. This provides the user with a more familiar and 'friendly' workspace environment. Developments in software compatibility are integrating the standard software packages in use on both central and local systems for mainstream applications such as databases.

Local area networks

A local area network is a means of linking together a collection of computer-based devices, within a limited geographical area, on a more or less equal basis. This equality makes the local area network (LAN) radically different from a terminal-based network, because each of the computer systems connected is an independent self-governing entity working in a co-operative relationship. Local area networks fall principally into two types:

— proprietary networks which are used to interconnect a number of computers and their peripherals of the same type, for example a network of IBMPC or Macintosh personal computers;

— standards-based networks which can interlink computer systems and devices whatever their type and specification, through the use of common network technology.

For both types of LAN, every device connected to the network must communicate through a uniform hardware interface and software protocol to achieve compatibility. Standardization of the communication process is therefore very important to the concept of local area networks. Since no one method of operation would be suitable for all possible needs, a number of alternative standards exist, reflected in the different types of LAN available. A local area network will typically be provided to support:

— resource sharing of expensive hardware resources, for example a colour printer, a high-speed modem, or a CDROM drive accessible to all nodes on the network;

— resource sharing of software and access to specialized facilities;

— file transfer and access to support the sharing of information between different users, and to provide wider access to central information while ensuring consistency by maintaining a single copy of the data;

— messaging and conferencing to enhance organizational communications and co-operative working;

The most commonly found use of proprietary local area networks is to interconnect IBM-PCs within a single site or building. There are broadly two types of PC-based local area network, distinguished by the operating system by which they are managed.

1. In peer-to-peer PC networks all the network nodes interrelate as equals, able to call on the services of other nodes and to offer their own at all times. This is an intuitively natural way of sharing resources, and is cheap and effective to implement for small workgroups.

2. In server-based PC networks, one or more network nodes act as a provider of services for the other client nodes. Clients can only call on the services of a server node, which is dedicated to this purpose; there are three main types of server: a file server dispenses data and program files across the network, either in whole or in part; a print server drives the printing devices and manages the print queues; and a communications server controls external links, such as facsimile machines, or modems.

Standards-based LANs

There are two industry wide standards for more broadly based local area networks, known as Ethernet and Token Ring.

Ethernet is the most widely installed local area network at the current time. This describes a specification for a LAN rather than an actual product; there are many implementations of Ethernet from a range of suppliers.

Ethernet aims to provide a high-speed network which gives all nodes stable and equal access to the network, in such a way as to prevent individual stations interfering with each other; and allowing a transmission to be addressed to individual nodes, a group of nodes, or the whole network community. The intention is that all Ethernet installations are compatible with each other, since they use the same set of protocols. The stations on an Ethernet are each linked directly to a main transmission channel in a bus topology. Stations may not transmit at the same time, but must wait for the channel to be free before sending; transmissions are broadcast to all nodes on the network, but only utilized by those stations to which the message is addressed.

There is a mechanism for the detection of collisions when stations broadcast together, which requires a station to rebroadcast after a random interval. Thus all stations are in contention for the channel and cannot be guaranteed a fixed rate of access. This method works well for small to medium size networks, where traffic is in irregular short bursts rather than at regular intervals, and

Ethernet therefore suits the typical office environment where user activity follows this pattern. Ethernet has a relatively high data rate of up to 10 Megabits per second (Mbps) and is able to support large data file transfers without undue disruption to the user. It does not, however, support voice and video transmission, because the nature of the access medium cannot guarantee the continuity necessary for voice or moving image. There are technical limitations to the size of Ethernet networks, both in length of cabling and in the amount of data traffic which can be supported.

The Token Ring network takes a different approach and as the form chosen by IBM for its own local area network has become more popular. The nodes are connected in a ring configuration, with each node receiving information from its 'upstream' neighbour and re-transmitting it to its nearest 'downstream' neighhour Each node, either originates its own transmission, passes on the data exactly as is received, or removes the data which is addressed to itself.

To control transmission collisions, each node has the opportunity to transmit in turn, governed by the passing of an electronic 'token' around the ring. The Token Ring thus provides for both an egalitarian 'round robin' access, and multiple priority levels for urgent messages. The method is self-governing to quite a high degree, and able to react dynamically to changing conditions.

IEEE standards

International standards development for local area networks has been co-ordinated by the Institute of Electrical and Electronic Engineers (IEEE) in the United States. This work is intended to develop a framework within which the major types of LAN can be encompassed rather than to specify one single standard for all requirements.

The standards are known by numerical, rather than product names, and cover both Ethernet and Token Ring style networks.

1. The 802.3 standard defines a broadcast bus-based network, which is effectively the same as the Ethernet type.
2. The 802.5 standard defines a token passing ring network similar to the IBM Token Ring local area network.

3. The 802.4 standard describes a token passing bus network, which combines features of the first two types.
4. The 802.6 standard defines a high-speed broadband network, better known as a metropolitan area network.

LANs Interconnections

As the local area network grows in size and complexity the amount of traffic increases, overloading the network and degrading response time and reliability. A number of devices have emerged to support both the partitioning of over-large LANs and the desirable interlinking of others.

1. A repeater carries messages between two sections of a single network, allowing it to be extended beyond the maximum cable limit.
2. A bridge is a station which is connected to two networks, through which the two LANs can exchange data frames. The networks must be using the same protocols so that they look like one logical network, but only traffic destined for nodes on the other network will pass over.
3. A router is a device for sending data frames between two dissimilar LANs, since the router can deal with both network types.
4. A gateway links a local area network to a different networking environment altogether, such as a wide area network.

The development of standards for local area networks is continuing with the emergence of newer technology and physical media. In particular, the use of fibre optics is having a substantial impact, potentially opening up the geographic and bandwidth limitations in this field to such an extent that distinctions between local and wide area networks are becoming less meaningful.

Wide area networks

In the wide area environment, the communications process is seen as a multi-stage process. Networks are constructed from point-to-point links between different nodes on a store and forward basis. Data transmission are passed from one node to the next, *en route,* with each node making its own routing decision based on matching the information which it holds in a routing table with the destination address on the data packet, and in the context of current network traffic conditions.

Control and management of the network is therefore distributed throughout, and not located in any single central point. The network can be extended by adding new connections between nodes and making appropriate updates to routing tables. There are likely to be alternative routes between nodes which can be used at different times. The relaying of data between nodes in this way requires the use of protocols to ensure correct delivery and protect against the corruption of transmissions *en route.*

The protocols normally operate both within the end systems and within the network relay nodes themselves. There are several alternative protocols suites which may be in use; however, all nodes on the network must be running the same protocols to communicate successfully, since this is the glue which binds the -disparate systems together.

As an indication, some common wide area protocols are:

— the X.25 protocols which have been developed for public telecommunications, and ensure international compatibility in this area; these have also been adopted in some private networks;

— the TCP/IP protocol suite, widely used in private networks and in the academic and research world.

Private data networks

Private data networks can be constructed from a number of different elements, as appropriate to requirements and conditions. They may be national or international in scope, and involve the co-ordination of several different network operators and administrations, using elements from:

— public telecommunications operators, in the form of leased data lines or use of the public data network;

— private network operators, including commercial long-haul network operators and satellite communications suppliers; independent local or wider scale data lines directly owned.

The leasing telecommunication lines

The leasing of dedicated digital data lines is an alternative to use of the public data network. These are private circuits, provided as a carrier by the telecommunications authority, but under the control of the organisation which is renting the line.

Leased lines are point to point connections, permanently linking one site with another, rather than dynamically switchable channels. Since they are leased at a fixed annual rate, the greater the use made of the line the more efficient it becomes.

Multiple rented private circuits are used by large organizations to create private networks, linking remote sites together on a point-to-point basis, or providing a high-speed network backbone for a high volume of traffic between main sites. In the United Kingdom BT provide a range of leased circuits with varying data carrying capacities:

— *Kilostream* and Kilostream N lines provide bulk data transmission at rates from 64 Kbps up to about 1 Megabit per second (Mbps);

— *Megastream* lines provide higher speeds of up to 2 Mbps;

— *Satstream* utilizes satellite capacity to offer point-to-multi-point connections over a wide geographical area.

The use of leased lines is a more secure and flexible option for the larger organization, which is able to deploy the systems and protocols which it finds most suitable, rather than having to conform to those used in public systems.

Telecommunications networks

There are three types of telecommunications network presently available for use for computer-based information networking; each of these represents a phase of the developmental efforts to improve services over several decades, using quite different technology and approaches.

Public switched telephone networks

This is an extensive network of cabling reaching into almost all inhabited parts of developed countries, and providing international connections worldwide. This made it attractive as an immediately available option for computer networking in its early stages. The PSTN network is designed for voice communication, and therefore requires the use of an interfacing data communication device, usually a modem, to be used.

The network makes use of circuit switching technology for the same reason, and is a rather noisy and unreliable channel, prone to errors and mis-connection. It is poorly suited to fast and reliable data transfer and depends on the end systems alone to maintain quality through the use of suitable protocols.

The PSTN makes inefficient use of the available carrying capacity because the circuit is idle when neither end system is transmitting but cannot be used by waiting nodes. Since a switched phone line is charged on a time and distance basis, regardless of the amount of traffic, it is not ideal for inter-computer communication over long distances.

Public data networks

The public data networks have been constructed specifically for the transmission of computer information, and cannot be used for voice conversations. They provide fast and reliable data transfer, more flexibility and international communications at a reasonable cost, since they are charged for by the amount of data transferred.

The advantages of packet switching are the following:

— there is no need for a direct physical connection between sender and receiver;

— information from different calls can then be interleaved on the network channels to make maximum use of the available bandwidth;

— the user, therefore, pays only for information actually transmitted, rather than for elapsed time regardless of the transfer activity;

— standard use of communication protocols facilitates the inter-connection of equipment from different manufacturers, operating at different data rates.

The X.25 protocol set is the standard for public packet switched networks. This is an open standard which is available for end systems as well as internally to the network.

Public data networks are mostly managed on a national basis with international connections between them, and so X.25 forms something approaching a global standard in this area. There are, however, two versions of the X.25 protocol; the latest 1988 version is not used by all public telecommunications operators. The public data network is essentially a store and forward network which operates at speeds fast enough to give the impression of a direct connection to the end user.

The network can be considered as an opaque entity—a 'cloud'—by the end systems which need only to specify an address for the remote end system which is being called, having no concern with the details of routing. The network 'cloud'- consists of a collection of packet switching exchanges (PSEs) which forward packets through the high-speed network from the local exchange to the destination PSE.

Integrated services digital networks

The development of public data networks for digital communications led to the existence of different networks for different purposes-one for voice, one for data-and requiring organizations using these systems to connect to both. A duplication of networks is undesirable, and also works against the integration of information types, for instance the co-ordination of voice, data, and image, which is increasingly needed to support multimedia information networking. Two development programmes in the telecommunications infrastructure provided the platform for the development of integrated services digital networks:

1. The digitization of the trunk network lines, the main arteries used by the network operator.
2. The replacement of electro-mechanical local telephone exchanges by digital switches, such as System X and System Y.

The ISDN aims to build a public network providing *end-to-end* digital connectivity which is capable of supporting a range of digital devices and services, both voice and non-voice, on the same basis. This allows users to send and receive data, text and image from computer systems as well as offering an enhanced telephone service. This is achieved over a single ISDN connection, so that one network may be used for all applications, at the same time as providing higher transmission speeds. The ISDN approach is to enable the existing local telephone circuitry-the 'local loop-to carry digital signals through the use of specialized equipment and adapters, rather than a wholesale and long-term replacement programme.

This requires the installation of suitable network connections in the customer premises, which acts as the interface to the digital network. Despite this fully digital transmission system it is still not possible to connect all computer equipment directly to the network, unless the equipment is designed or adapted to work-with the ISDN system. Access to the ISDN network is available at two different capacity rates, known as basic rate and primary rate.

The access rate refers to the number of logical channels which are available on a single ISDN connection. Each of these channels constitutes a circuit which is independently usable by different information media, and can be switched to different destination points.

The Basic Access Rate provides two *bearer* channels and one *data* channel, and for this reason is otherwise known as 213 + D. Each of the bearer channels can simultaneously carry a separate information stream, at a transfer rate of 64 Kbps-for example, one for a voice call and the other for data.

The Primary Access Rate gives a higher number of bearer channels, although the exact number is variable between countries—the United Kingdom, Europe and Australia supply 30 bearer channels to the user in one ISDN connection (known as 30B + D); in the United States, Japan and South East Asia 23 channels are used. 30B + D gives an overall data rate of some 2 Mbps (the equivalent to a BT Megastream leased line) and necessitates the use of extra equipment at the subscriber premises to manage the multiple channels.

Potential benefits from the use of ISDN are the following:

— all 30 ISDN connections can be switched to different locations;

— clearer calls and more reliable data transfers, with less line noise;

— the ability to send two information streams to the same locations, to support remote co-operative working; for example, two users might discuss over the phone the contents of a computer screen which can be transferred between their terminals;

— enabling domestic services, such as home shopping and banking, online database access, security, and control services for the home;

— feasible desktop videoconferencing;

— providing a better infrastructure for teleworking, for example by providing a gateway to an office LAN for home-based workers.

Frame relay networks

Frame relay networks technologies are in development which may threaten to overwhelm ISDN before its full potential is reached. These involve the use of high-speed packet switching on high bandwidth networks which will offer much greater information transmission capabilities than the present public data networks. Frame relay networks are made possible by use of less noisy transmission media, such as fibre optic cable, in the network infrastructure, exploiting this greater reliability to simplify the protocols necessary and thus speed up the transmission process.

Integrated broadband networks

Integrated broadband networks are sometimes referred to as broadband ISDN (B-ISDN) systems and will also exploit the advantages of fibre optic to offer a dramatically enhanced communication facility, far more powerful than exists at present and able to deliver a wider range of services more effectively.

The intention of developing integrated broadband communications systems is to provide a single network for all services, which can be flexibly and dynamically configured according to individual circumstances and priorities. Digital networks allow both data, voice and image to be sent along the same connection, but these information types have different desirable transmission characteristics.

Data and text require a high degree of accuracy, since the quality of the received information is more easily affected by corruption, but are more tolerant of short transmission delays. Voice and the moving image, on the other hand, are more tolerant of errors since these can be interpreted by human interpretation, but are more susceptible to variations in transmission delays. Existing or narrowband ISDN circuits do not have a high degree of flexibility in adjusting to these varying demands: for instance, a voice call does not use the full capacity of a 64 Kbps channel, but the spare cannot be freed up for use by others during a session.

Broadband networks aim to overcome such problems by using a universal fast packet switching technique for all information streams, and allocating 'bandwidth on demand' rather than relying on fixed bandwidth channels. Two rates have been proposed for B-ISDN: a basic rate service with a digital access rate of 155 Mbps, and a primary rate service at 622 Mbps, although the full specifications for these have yet to be defined.

A technique known as the Asynchronous Transfer Mode (ATM) is used to transfer the data. This divides the data stream into cells, which are smaller than X.25 packets in size, and can travel through the network at a faster rate. Since the channel is more reliable, quality control is performed at each end of the link and not by each intermediate network switch as well. This ATM approach is particularly suitable for information activity which is inherently 'bursty' in nature.

For example, a service would be able to ensure fast delivery of high definition images, and then free the channel for other use during the reading and thinking time in which the user is not generating any network activity. This will allow the development of true multimedia information services.

Developments in the wider networking field are increasing aiming to deliver faster data transfer rates, on integrated networks which make no distinction between information types.

As the amount of electronic information available across networks grows exponentially, and the sophistication of end-user computing equipment encourages the sharing of information in more intensive forms, network infrastructures respond with the ability to communicate sophisticated forms fast enough to make actual use of the network transparent to the user. At the organizational level, local area networks are also undergoing technical developments which increase their speed and potential for the delivery of more sophisticated and high-powered information applications.

A situation in which these applications can make use of the network 'on demand' in a flexible manner which can respond to changes in circumstance is foreseeable. There is, however, much effort required to make this a reality; the current situation reflects a confusing picture of many alternative networking options which conflict and compete with each other, and which are poorly suited to widespread interconnection between different types of network. The concept of connectivity stresses the importance of this ability to interconnect networks and information networking applications in a reliable and effective manner, and without the need for equipment which is difficult to obtain, install, and use, and soon redundant.

6

Towards Open Systems

The concepts of open systems are now widely accepted in principle, with many believing that the OSI model forms the underlying solution to connectivity problems. In practice, however, the actual take-up of OSI in terms of working products has been slower than at first anticipated. The slow pace of standards development tends to prolong uncertainty amongst end-users, and discourages suppliers from manufacturing OSI products on a large scale due to the lack of a mass market.

The lower network-dependent levels of the OSI model are well established in both local and wide area networks; the upper levels are much less well supported with few general or specialized products in most areas. The second problem facing OSI products is that of conformance testing, to ensure that inter-operability standards are met. These are relatively new, and although normally carried out by an independent third party, do not necessarily guarantee full compatibility; variations within the paper standard mean that compliant products will not always work with each other, still further undermining user confidence and acceptance.

The interchange technology should allow a user working on one system to use an application on another system, without concern with data formats; the long-term goal is to allow network users to co-operate seamlessly with each other, regardless of physical location or equipment. A common framework for networked information interchange must incorporate generic application problems, such as remote database access, file transfer and interpersonal messaging, in a way that separates the local form of the application from the interchange aspects, enabling flexible variations in the former while standardizing on the latter.

De facto and de jure standards may emerge from two main sources. De facto standards are those which derive from the use and popularity of easily available products, through a process in which the most successful become widely accepted as industry standards. Proprietary standards from single computer manufacturers (such as IBM's Systems Network Architecture) fall into this group; while having the advantage of the backing of a major interest group, their future development is unpredictable, and they are 'closed' systems in that the full specification for the standard is not published but kept as a trade secret. De facto standards may also emerge through adoption by a number of different product developers, and have the general support of a wider range of users who may also participate in the standards making process itself. This type of process is likely to be founded on widespread availability, and may be stimulated by an initial development, or adoption, of the standard in government administration projects. This has been the case with the TCP/IP communications protocols, which are widely used in industry, government and education (particularly in the United States) and form one approach to the 'opening' of computer systems to each other.

De jure standards are those which emerge from an organized, usually public, programme sponsored by governmental or international initiative, emerging from an open debate over several years; by their nature, these developments are more speculative in nature, formulating paper specifications rather than products. The successful take-up of the standard may depend on the willingness of private manufacturers to build conformable products, or on the degree to which the standard can be imposed by regulation.

The CCITT recommendations for telecommunications, for example, can be reinforced by regulations governing approval of equipment for connection to public networks. Standards for software in computer systems cannot be regulated in this way, but can be encouraged by making them mandatory in private tenders for substantial government information system projects. The main international efforts towards the specification of a framework for open, intercommunicating, systems has been the work done under the aegis of the International Standards Organization (ISO) and known as Open Systems Interconnection. Although this is a long-term programme intended to take effect slowly, at the present time the ISO Open Systems model has had more influence in Europe than elsewhere.

Open systems interconnection (OSI) aims to develop a framework for the development and approval of computer networking standards that provides communications-based user services which support inter-working with computer systems from different manufacturers, in different geographical locations. This framework defines a conceptual and functional model for supporting multi vendor, multimedia and multi-software networking by formalizing and delineating the problems involved in sustaining it, and structuring them within an open architecture.

The basic idea of OSI is not to invent a completely new set of protocols where adequate ones already exist, or to impose any one single approach or technology, but instead to acknowledge existing protocols by placing them within the framework of the model according to open architecture principles. In this way, OSI functions as a focus for co-ordinating standards development, and depends on achieving a consensus view from all interested parties.

The International Standards Organization is a worldwide standards agency, based in Geneva, for the establishment of scientific and technical standards. It is composed of representatives from a wide range of other organizations, especially the national standards institutes—for example the British Standards Institute and the US equivalent, ANSI (the American National Standards Institute)— and works in collaboration with other standards bodies, such as the CCITT international telecommunications authority, the US-based Institute of Electrical and Electronic Engineers, the European Computer Manufacturers Association, and professional groupings representing the user population.

The organization progresses its work through a web of committees, subcommittees and working groups, developing and adapting standards through lengthy consultation processes. Before being formally adopted as an International Standard, a specification will pass through working paper, draft proposal and draft international standard phases, with public comment and feedback at each stage; ten years is a not untypical timespan for this process. The basic OSI reference model was formally adopted in 1983, and has since been elaborated for particular task types and application areas. The mission of OSI is described as:

— to specify a universally applicable logical communications structure;

— to encourage different users to communicate with each other by compatible implementation of communication features;

— to serve as a reference point in the development of new communication services;

— to enable the steady evolution of applications through the flexible incorporation of technical advances and the expansion of user requirements.

The open systems interconnection model does not impose a single standard, but incorporates a collection of existing standards, placing them in the context of an abstract model of the communications process. Compliance with the model is intended to ensure functional equivalence between computer systems.

The term system is here used to denote a collection of computers, software, peripherals, and human operators which have information transfer capabilities as an autonomous whole—that is, a tightly linked computer network as much as a single computer installation. OSI is therefore a standard for network-to-network communications. Given the tremendous diversity of needs and options in this area, a single universal protocol is not possible. The OSI approach is to group functionally similar protocols into a set of layers, each of which represents a particular class of service available in open systems. The basic reference model defines each of these layers by specifying both the *functionality* of each layer and the *interface* between adjacent layers. The specification of the functionality within any particular layer defines what is to be done rather than *how* it should be done. The way in which these functions are implemented in software programs therefore can vary between different products, although the outcomes should remain compatible.

The specification of the interface between layers ensures that the information which is received and passed on between software modules is in a standard form. The functional layers are stacked in a pre-defined order to form organized and structured communication tasks. Each layer provides a set of services to the next highest layer in the stack on demand; to be able to provide these it receives a set of services from the next lowest layer in the stack. Since each layer is providing its own set of specialized tasks (specified as the functionality of the layer), it acts as a user in relation to the layer beneath, requesting services from it but knowing nothing about how they are achieved. Data passes up and down the stack using the standard interfaces as a conduit, with each layer adding control information relevant to its own specialized tasks in the overall communication process, and passing the package on.

An analogy might be a set of Russian dolls, in which the larger doll encapsulates a smaller one. In OSI terms the original nugget of data is passed down and encapsulated by larger control messages as it passes through each layer on the transmitting system; on receipt the process is reversed, and the larger containers are stripped off as the message passes back up the stack of equivalent layers on the receiving system.

The model deals only with the logical structure of the communications process and says nothing about how this is to be physically implemented. Since each layer is acting as a self-contained module within its own boundaries, an individual implementation of layer tasks in any particular system can change without having an overall effect on the communication strategy, as long as it conforms to the logical requirements.

Software modules can then be changed in individual systems to accommodate changes in user needs and network technology, as long as the new version continues to provide the same set of services through a standard interface. In the OSI model the overall communications tasks are partitioned into seven layers, with no overlap between them. Each layer communicates with to equivalent 'peer' layer on the remote system by exchanging messages on matters for which it alone is responsible. This is actually achieved through using the services provided by subordinate layers, but each individual layer works as though it were speaking directly with its peer in the remote system. This peer-to-peer communication is made possible by the standard boundaries between layers which are the same on both linked systems. The seven layers in the model fall into two main sections. The three uppermost layers are primarily concerned with the applications communicating via the linked systems, and with organizing the provision of services to human users.

The three lowest layers are concerned with the technical transmission problems of sending data across networks; the fourth layer (the transport layer) acts as an interface between these two broad tasks. The three lower layers are supported in both the end systems and the network mediating between them; the upper layers are in the end systems only.

The physical layer controls the actual physical connection between the two systems, the hardware standards used, and the method of data transmission, working at the level of the individual data bit. The data link layer provides error handling and flow control, and works at the level of the data frame. The network layer controls both routing decisions and the relaying of data packets through intermediate systems, concealing from the upper layers the particular path through the network which is being used.

The transport layer is the first to be primarily concerned with end-to-end operation, concerned with quality of service and ensuring a reliable connection for the upper layers. There are five different classes of service available from the transport layer, including connection-oriented and connectionless services. The end systems must agree which class is in use for the session before exchange of data can commence. The session layer is responsible for setting up an individual session between two systems, and managing the inter-system dialogue on behalf of the higher layers; for instance, synchronizing the information flows between the applications, and allowing activities to be started, abandoned, paused, and restarted correctly.

The presentation layer negotiates how data is to be presented to the application, dealing with character sets and codes, agreeing to exchange data in a shared common format. End systems which use different information coding sets (such as ASCII or EBCDIC) can use a special open transfer syntax notation called Abstract Syntax Notation 1 (ASN. 1). The application layer, the topmost layer of the OSI stack, is responsible for interfacing with the local end system and ultimately for supplying direct network services to the user. In an open systems environment, all lower level OSI functions can only be accessed through the application layer, and not directly.

The application layer is not a user application in its own right, but rather handles the semantics of the communication process in the same way that the presentation layer handles the syntax. It has specialized elements for different generic applications, such as file transfer and electronic mail, which interface with proprietary packages for these applications installed on the local end system. For example, a person would send and receive electronic mail through the same package which they normally use on their own system; this local package translates the mail into terms acceptable to the OSI e-mail application layer element, which in turn initiates the setting up and management of the appropriate communication characteristics by the next layers, and so on down the stack. For the transfer to be successful, the receiving system must be able to support the same kinds of action, in reverse.

As a logical model of the whole communication process, each layer is effectively split across the two end systems which are exchanging information; the interaction between pairs of layers determines the particular characteristics of an individual connection during the time it takes place. Each layer is able to 'speak' directly to its peer about its own concerns, even though there is only one actual physical connection, controlled by the lowest layer; and even though each layer may in fact be implemented by different products from different manufacturers. There is a basic level of functionality specified for each layer which ensures an essential core of services across all implementations, known as the kernel functional unit. Each layer may also offer extra functions in the shape of additional activities, also grouped together as functional units.

The basic level of service for each layer is mandatory for working in an open-systems environment; additional functional units are named after the type of service they offer, and can be optional, so that individual OSI products may contain only some of those that are possible.

Application layer standards request service from lower layers in the form of functional units. One of the responsibilities of the session layer is to establish whether an equivalent set of functional units to those first requested (including the optional ones) is available on the system which is being called, to negotiate an acceptable common environment within which the exchange can take place. Not all combinations of options within the OSI framework will be compatible with each other. For example, the OSI model includes both a connectionless and a connection-oriented type of service, enabling a local area network to interconnect with an X.25 service for example. However, an upper layer working in connection-oriented mode cannot co-operate with a peer which works only in connectionless mode.

The application layer in the OSI strategy is the one most closely associated with the movement of information, rather than data, between users on systems. The layer supports particular types of applications by defining an application agent for each type. The range is growing as more types are specified, and includes both generic and specialised applications. Generic applications are those which are widely used in many different contexts, such as file transfer, terminal access, and electronic mail, and were the earliest to be defined. Specialized applications are those which are relevant to quite narrow areas of activity; for instance in the library field, these include inter-system communications for information retrieval and interlibrary loan.

File transfer is one of the more difficult problems in data networking, since the way in which files are stored and handled varies considerably between different manufacturers. The File Transfer and Access Method provides a reliable transfer of all or parts of data files from one system to another, even if the file structures and access methods are different, and is guaranteed to result in a correct copy, or a message that the activity has failed with an automatic restart. FTAM also provides the ability to change the characteristics and contents of a file remotely from a different computer system.

In a networked environment, there are many different terminal types from different manufacturers which may potentially wish to connect to an information system, so that the software running on a host system has the problem of recognising and responding to these different terminal types. This can be quite a significant problem, especially with IBM mainframe hosts, and may require the user to operate different terminal emulation programs for different hosts.

For example, the ability to use online catalogues across a network can be severely limited by the idiosyncrasies of terminal access and often leads to a 'lowest common denominator' approach to screen presentation design. Ideally, the user should not need to be aware of terminal characteristics in using networked systems.

The Virtual Terminal (VT) standard is designed to allow host computer systems to communicate successfully with a variety of terminals by separating the user application from the terminal display. A virtual terminal software product would therefore be in two parts, one part installed on the host system with the user application, and the other part on the particular terminal or workstation in use, co-operating together through a standard protocol. This allows a user to retain the same 'look and feet' of the interface across different host applications.

Job Transfer and Manipulation allows a user to send processing tasks to a different computer without having to know the details of its control language. Although this is not widely used at present, in the long term it is hoped that JTM will support automatic scheduling and sharing of tasks between all available resources on the network, so that this is not apparent to the user—in effect, the user would be to able to use the full combined power of the network as though it were a single computer system.

Remote Database Access supports the ability to query relational databases across a network in a standard manner. Since the relational data model is well defined, there is an underlying consistency to different packages available and a widely used database query language, the Standard Query Language (SQL), which is an ISO standard in its own right. Remote Database Access is broadly compatible with the SOL language.

The concept of the OSI model is to design a framework for the inclusion of many possible standards (for example, the major local area network standards and the X.25 packet switching service) within a common functional structure. Within this structure there are different possible options for building up a communications process from different combinations of elements within and between layers; not all possible combinations are internally feasible or compatible. To simplify the model for use with a particular user context, specialized versions or subsets have been identified by interested user groups for use with their own applications. These are known as functional profiles, a thread of standards running down through all the layers of the model, but not encompassing all facets across the breadth of all levels.

A functional profile may include a limited set of options within itself, and can act as a detailed specification to which computer suppliers can build specialized products with confidence of user acceptance in that particular field. The specification of functional profiles is also a means by which large powerful bodies can influence the rate of take up of OSI standards. One of the first user groups to work out such a functional profile was the UK government, which now makes use of the Government OSI Profile (GOSIP) mandatory in government information system projects wherever it is appropriate.

Equivalent work is being undertaken by the European standards organizations to define compatible profiles in an EC context, and to harmonize these with the GOSIP work. The United States government has taken similar steps by making OSI a feature of federal information projects. The MAP/TOP profile has been defined by General Motors and Boeing for manufacturing and technical office automation.

A similar project is in progress in the library communications field, with close involvement from national libraries and representatives of major national library and information interest groups. The particular nature of bibliographic information, the primary requirements of those who would be earliest users of open systems, and the context of existing bibliographic information systems into which OSI would fit, determine the greater appropriateness of some elements of the model and highlight the need to develop more specialized elements as yet unrepresented.

The National Library of Canada has taken a strong lead in much of this work, which has been progressing slowly over the last decade. Application standards for information retrieval between bibliographic information systems which use different command languages, and for the handling of automated interlibrary loan requests.

The OSI approach has been to analyse, incorporate, and specify the entire networking process in all its aspects, with the hope of defining a *de jure* standard to which future developments will conform. The slow and meticulous pace of this work is not well suited to keeping in step with new developments in technology or new demands from network users.

An alternative to the OSI scheme which has achieved more dominance in recent years are the two protocols known as Transmission Control Protocol and Internet Protocol—which together form the more easily referred to TCP/IP. TCP/IP was originally developed for the

United States military computer network ARPANET under government auspices, and has been recommended for government use in information systems projects for many years. It is not a rigorously defined specification in the same way as the OSI model, and does not cover the same breadth of ground; in fact, it is now rather old and unsophisticated as an approach to networking problems.

However, since the specification for the standard is published and in the public domain, it has been widely taken up by commercial manufacturers and others, and in this sense is considered as an 'open standard', the details of which are freely available. Due to this widespread availability and comparatively straightforward approach TCP/IP is in wide use in both wide area and local area networks, and a number of user-oriented applications have been developed and adapted in response to perceived user need. New applications are not required to go through such a formal process of approval as OSI equivalents, so that the time scales between development and installation are much reduced. In this sense, TCP/IP forms a *de facto* standard with well-tested and well-understood applications, which can be put into practice immediately, with a strong appeal to the more pragmatically minded as a flexible working solution to internetworking problems which has evolved heuristically from real needs rather than from paper specifications.

Although it is not without its own problems, which become more obvious as the protocol becomes more widely used, TCP/IP has been strongly championed by some as an alternative to the OSI approach in the so-called 'protocol wars'. The recent astonishing growth of the US-based Internet network, which uses TCP/IP to bind together a very large number of subnetworks, has given some credence to this notion at least in the short term.

The protocols fall into two parts. The Internet Protocol (IP) provides routing services broadly equivalent to (but not matching) the network layer 3 in the OSI model. The Transmission Control Protocol (TCP) deals with the equivalent of OSI transport layer 4 and session layer 5 functions, providing both a connectionless and a connection-oriented service. Neither of these, however, is a complete implementation of the functionality defined in these OSI layers, and does not divide the functions between layers in the same way; and so is not compatible.

There is no OSI-style application layer to provide the interface linking with user applications, and so these functions must be produced separately for individual systems and will vary accordingly. There are, however, a few generic application processes available which perform some equivalent functions to OSI application layer standards for the main user activities which take place on a network.

The *file transfer protocol (ftp)* supports access to and transfer of files between a user and a host system across a network, for both text and binary (program) type files, and in some cases bit-mapped image files. From a user's point of view, the protocol consists of a set of commands which reflect a Unix system environment. These allow a user to open a connection to a remote host on a TCP/IP network by giving the IP network address to identify the called system; to read directories and filenames once logged-in to the host; to transfer files from the remote host to the home system; to transfer files in the opposite direction if the host system allows this; and to close the connection once the transaction is completed.

The *Telnet* protocol supports interactive access to information applications on a remote computer by emulating a standard terminal. The telnet application runs on the home system, and disguises some terminal-specific features, allowing a user to log-in to the remote system and use it as though there were a direct connection. The *Simple Mail Transfer Protocol (SMTP)* provides interpersonal messaging between systems running different electronic mail packages, providing a standard format through which messages are generated and by which they can be received.

The OSI model, as a portfolio of standards and an architecture that binds them together, is often judged a more comprehensive and long-term approach, capable of handling a large number of interlinked systems with seamless access to all points, as well as providing better security, back-up, and recovery mechanisms.

The experience gained from design and use of TCP/IP has fed into the open-systems development process, and the longer time-scales have enabled more considered and participative decision-making. There is some uncertainty about the future of both approaches, with TCP/IP strongly supported in North America (partly due to its use on the Internet) and OSI most strongly favoured by efforts towards European network integration. There is no straightforward compatibility between the two, and in many situations both sets of protocols can coexist together on the same network. This can happen at three levels:

A dual-stack configuration, where both sets are present together, but do not interconnect. This implies two parallel sets of applications, requiring the user to know which one to select for certain conditions, and complicating network administration and maintenance.

A gateway which links two systems using different protocols. This arrangement can make transparent conversions (e.g. from SMTP to X.400 mail), but some of the power deriving from specialized applications can be lost in the process. The building of hybrid stacks, with OSI top layers over TCP/IP lower layers, or vice versa; such a network can only directly communicate with those who have the same arrangement.

The OSI approach clearly separates user interface issues from network communication issues, so that standardization on the networking component does not prevent the design of different user interfaces for different user groups on the local end system. This movement is founded on the Unix operating system, which provides the one example of a non-proprietary computer operating system that is not bound to any particular make of machine, but is available and used across the range of hardware platforms.

Although not noted for its ease of use, Unix is flexible and adaptable to circumstances, and the core facilities are able to be presented through a range of different user interface shells. Unfortunately, there are a number of different competing versions of Unix, with various interests vying to establish one in particular as the standards version. The Open Software Foundation is an association of computer industry bodies, including IBM, and favouring a version known as Motif; the alternative, Unix International, includes AT&T and champions the Unix System V version. Many of these manufacturers are also shareholders in the X/Open corporation, an international organization attempting to group the confusing variety of open-systems standards under a common Umbrella through the development of a common applications environment.

7

Public Service Networking

This chapter deals with the areas of information networking within the community context, ranging from voluntary community networks aiming to provide the citizen with general information for everyday life, to sophisticated systems for urban management and health care. Each of these areas has seen a growth in activity in recent years, as access to information becomes a more important factor in daily decision-making, whether at the individual or organizational level.

Recently, the ubiquitous spread of network access and microcomputers have encouraged the development of more pro-active forms, under the aegis of local governments or local voluntary not-for-profit groups (particularly in the United States), which aim to provide the framework for community action which supports two-way networking, rather than the simple one-way passive consumption of display only systems.

Viewdata systems have been installed in public libraries since the early 1980s, following the emergence of the British Telecom Prestel public information system. This is now a rather outdated and unsophisticated system, and is not amenable towards tailoring for local community information. The late 1980s saw the growing use by public libraries of private viewdata systems which are developed and sometimes managed by commercial enterprises on behalf of their clients; these can be customized for individual applications and managed as a closed user group facility, offering specific information targeted at a well-defined user group. A recent survey showed that 40 public library authorities use a private viewdata system, and that this use is replacing that of Prestel (and broadcast teletext services such as Ceefax and Oracle) both in terms of numbers of systems and in overall usage by the public.

Added to the local focus in information content, there is also the advantage that some local authorities adopt private viewdata as an internal corporate information system, allowing the library to make use of any spare capacity. The Electronic Public Information Network (previously the Local Authority Videotex Association) acts as a forum for channelling ideas and advice in videotex, investigating hardware and software issues, and developing applications for community information needs. This has some 46 local authority members and a number of other public sector and private organizations.

In the context of local government authorities rather than just public libraries, a survey by the Society of Information Technology Managers in 1992 revealed that 19% of UK local authorities already have public access terminals installed, and that a further 14% planned to do so in the near future. These were installed in venues as diverse as libraries, council buildings, and shopping precincts, containing information on:

— local organizations and events;

— details of general practitioners;

— transport information;

— tourist information, including accommodation listings;

— information services aimed at local economic

development, for example EC information on legislation, calls for tender, potential European business partners;

— one-stop enquiry shops, staffed by assistants able to make use of the local authority computer network to answer information enquiries on council services and activities.

Since community information needs do not exactly match local authority boundaries, there is a growing tendency to combine together localized services to form geographically wider-ranging information systems. Doncaster Metropolitan Borough in South Yorkshire, for example, has developed a successful viewdata service known as DONFACTS, giving details of employment vacancies, and local events and activities; in 1989 the South Yorkshire Libraries Viewdata Information Service was formed to create a regional service from this and other participants in the area.

An alternative to Integrated library system module is the use of a purpose-designed module within an integrated library system such as GEAC. This has the advantage of allowing the information to be directly controlled by the library authority itself, and to integrate it with the other activities and information services offered by the public library.

Community information, for instance, may appear as one option on an Online Public Access Catalogue terminal, along with information relating to library holdings, updated and maintained in the same way. An example of this approach is the CINDEX system, the Camden Community Information Network Directory and Exchange, developed from the GEAC Local Information System. The use of an integrated system gave the possibility of direct access to the information, rather than requiring the user to traverse the 'tree' structure of menus typical of viewdata systems, with the use of various access points; and offered the functionality to manipulate and print subsets of the information base as specialized products. Once again, maintenance of this system requires co-operation with neighbouring areas, since urban information requirements are not constrained by administrative borders.

A recent development in the provision of community information has been the growth in co-operative host systems which, instead of building up a centralized bank of information for dissemination to users at terminal access points, concentrate rather on building a facilitating infrastructure which offers a framework for diverse groups to build and maintain their own information systems and services. Host systems offer general facilities for creating local information files, the exchange of information between specific small user groups, and the creation of developmental projects and workshops, as well as more traditional services such as access to external databases.

The Manchester Host system uses an internationally available communications software system more widely known as Geo-net, which is installed in some 40 countries around the world; Manchester Host is directly linked to several of these other Hosts in Europe (including Eastern and Central Europe), Russia and the USA through the international telecommunications networks.

The Host is accessible to its subscribers through use of a phone line, PC and modem. Services include:

— *electronic mail* to other Host subscribers internationally, and to telex and facsimile services, and X.400 mail, as well as gateways to other e-mail systems, such as BT Gold, MCI Mail and Telemail;

— *data facilities* for the creation of bulletin boards, computer conferencing, and file exchange, and for the uploading of data to create new local online database services;

— *online database access* through a common searching language to external databases in both the commercial and voluntary sectors, for example to FT Profile, and the Amnesty International bibliographic database on human rights, together with an integrated billing mechanism which removes the need for each user to have individual subscription to specific database hosts;

— *network access* to other systems, such as Easynet, the Internet, GreenNet, and APC GreenNet.

The Host approach assumes that users are potential information providers as well as consumers of information, encouraging an active participation in creating new applications and making contributions to existing ones. This led the Host initiative to borrow the idea of electronic village halls from the telecottages movement, and establish these in localized areas of Manchester, offering new technology facilities and training for particular groups, organized and managed by these groups themselves: for example electronic village halls have been established by women's groups, for small local business, and for the local Bangladeshi community.

As well as supporting greater participation for the individual in the information age through a philosophy of low-cost access and distributed processing, the Host approach has been to promote private and public sector partnership for the development of specific project initiatives for closed user groups. This involves cooperation between local government, employers and businesses, higher education institutes, trade unions, and non-governmental organizations, working on projects to extend the ISDN network and the consequent development of broadband information services, the extension of electronic data interchange (EDI) to smaller enterprises, and the development of a communications park for business. A number of closed user groups built around specific cooperative needs have evolved including:

— the Manchester Chinese Information Centre, supporting document exchange in Chinese script to the local ethnic community;

— the Manchester Business School, which uses the system to communicate with similar institutions on an international footing;

— the Manchester Asian Trading Network to improve trading links between local Asian business and suppliers in Bangladesh;

— the Manchester Design Community, in which smaller enter prises co-operate on bidding for larger contracts as a consortium.

On a wider geographic level, links with other European cities allow for greater co-operation in trans-regional development initiatives. GeoNet systems are existing in Berlin, Athens, Moscow, Seville, Sofia, Siberia, Cyprus, Crete, Poland, and Finland among others. The European and international linkages are likely to develop more strongly in the longer term, encouraged by the recent bid by Manchester to host the Olympic Games.

The Host system brings together a diversity of community issues and related information activities focused on a locality. A range of networks have also sprung up to link together groups and organizations working in similar Areas, though geographically dispersed. The 'networking' term is sometimes used rather freely in this context; some examples of these are closer to centralized database systems which offer remote access to users. Volnet, for example, is a central database host, providing a route to information for workers in the voluntary and community sectors at low-cost. The database offers online access to a bibliographic database, backed up by a photocopy-based document supply service, and to information on research projects and the details of UK parliamentary candidates.

GreenNet provides a similar service for non-governmental organizations and individuals working with ecological and environmental issues, giving access to a range of computer conferences and resources, with a common structure to the location of information files in the network. APC GreenNet links together progressive organizations with an interest in the development of information communication for social change, such as Amnesty International. A range of similar networking initiatives exist, some short- and some longer lived. These can operate at a purely national level, or work on an international scale, for example the *TUDIC* network which supports co-operation and the sharing of information between trade unions in Sweden, Denmark, and the UK.

While many of the existing community networks in the USA have evolved from local initiatives, stemming either from citizen groups or public authority organizations, recent years have seen the emergence of commercial organizations piloting or operating information networks directed at local users on a for-profit basis. These organizations make information produced by, others available whilst profiting from advertising through the network facilities. *American CitiNet* operates this service bureau arrangement, with particular customer bases in Omaha and Boston. The *regional Bell operating companies,* the US regional telecommunication suppliers, are beginning to offer gateway facilities to information providers who are then able to recover their costs from information users through the normal billing arrangements of the Bell companies. A number of local government agencies are providing information and services in this way.

As well as communicating with clients of their services, local government authorities have used information networking as a means of co-ordinating and delivering the services for which they are responsible. There is an increasing recognition for the need to integrate and consolidate the single-focus information sets that are incomplete and incompatible, or fragmented across departmental and administrative boundaries, in order to deliver services effectively and support local development.

The networking of databases and administrative systems increases access to information and forms a platform for the development of more powerful and sophisticated integrated systems. Local access to council services and information is effected by networking local branch offices and the creation of information points at which the public can find out about a range of council services, such as housing, employment, transport, and trading standards, together in one place; and can make specific enquiries about their individual progress, in areas such as payment of council tax or council house repairs.

Information access points such as these can be queried by telephone, and in some areas have taken the form of mobile services linked to a central computer system. This growth in the integration of information systems is linked to the development of new forms of service based on emerging information technology. Geographical information systems are a prime example of this, since much of the work of local authorities is spatially related.

Different information bases, for example, may contain mapping data on the location of gas, electricity, and water utility pipes, property ownership and land use, and demographic information for strategic planning. Although these may be distributed over different locations and agencies, their integration across a network offers the opportunity for more advanced services: for example, transport information management systems which link traffic flows with highway maintenance and emergency services; or demographic planning with library development and community analysis to determine information needs.

Local authorities are increasingly providing information services linked to local economic development. While the Manchester Host is one important example of a far-reaching approach to this, more traditional information services include access to European databases for information on European Commission tenders and contracts, EC legislation, and searching for business partners in other EC countries. Staffordshire County Council, for example, is one of 25 areas connected to a European network for the communication of this type of information.

A similar requirement encourages the integration of information access between different service delivery agencies. Recent changes in UK legislation have reinforced this trend, particularly with regard to the delivery of personal social services; this is one area in which the local authority is presented with a lead role as an enabler for their delivery.

The Child Protection Register maintained by social service departments, for example, is in some cases available to accident and emergency departments of local hospitals in electronic form. The recent Care in the Community Act presupposes the exchange of information between social service departments and community health authorities.

The National Disability Information Project, formed under the auspices of the Department of Health, is a further influence developing this role for public service agencies. One of the pilot projects is the GUiDe system under development in Gloucestershire between the Gloucester and Cheltenham Health Authorities and the County Social Services Department. This deals with information for elderly and disabled people, and gives networked access to health professionals in hospitals, voluntary organizations, health centres, and social services offices. Another project is based at Gateshead Libraries and Arts Service, well known for its innovative viewdata-based home shopping experiment.

The Gateshead Disability Information project aims to make information from the council on disability available in various complementary forms—sound, text and video—of the user's own choosing, and through a variety of delivery mechanisms.

There is a similar requirement for local government and local agencies to interwork with central government in an online networked environment, dealing with electronic information, often driven by central government directly. The Department for Education, for instance, uses electronic data interchange (EDI) to communicate with school educators on statistics and teachers' pensions matters, and similar arrangements for transport and trading standards are likely to emerge.

Quasi-governmental organizations also have information exchange requirements with local areas, and as these bodies automate their information resources and archives they are developing online access arrangements to replace manual administration for remote users. Increasingly, these applications demand more sophisticated information exchange facilities and broadband network links to accommodate heavy data transfer loads and multimedia information types. A recent example is the MONARCH system developed by the Royal Commission on Historical Monuments of England, an electronic version of the National Monuments Record. The online version of this gives remote access for about 200 users to some 6 million items of information on ancient monuments, including graphic images with hypertext linkages as well as text-based searching.

The information is used by local government for planning purposes, by English Nature for conservation decisions, and by the National Trust for property management, and will in the future be linked to geographical information systems for map-based searching and retrieval.

Local authorities have traditionally been involved in the direct provision of services, including information services and information related to other activities. As information becomes more and more important as a basic commodity for daily life, many see local government as having a role in the planning and development of a local information infrastructure, aimed at facilitating the integration and sharing of information from many sources and encouraging a policy of common access and citizen participation as well as enabling local economic and community development.

The growing interest in teleworking and the establishment of service centres for telecommunications seem to call naturally on the support of local government, and this approach has found heavy investment in Japan, for example, where telecommuting has formed a major plank in the development of regional information systems; although in the UK, at the present time, there has not been the same display of interest.

As changes in society, and in the structure and nature of organizations create changes in work patterns and habits for those who work in them or use their products and services, the change towards client-focused rather than organization-focused services may offer opportunities for a new role for local government in this area.

Perhaps the first developments in this area can be seen in the recent creation of 'One stop shops' providing information, counselling, and advice support services for local businesses, established under the auspices of the Department for Trade and Industry. These are mostly based on joint arrangements between Training and Enterprise Councils, chambers of commerce and local authorities, taking different forms in different areas. Six main areas have been selected as the first pilots. These include urban areas such as Birmingham, where the Birmingham Libraries business information service is involved, to larger rural areas such as Hertfordshire, where the Hertis Information and Research consultancy and Hertfordshire Libraries are involved in the feasibility study.

Several of the development programmes started by the Commission for the European Community programmes are aimed at the development of networking as a supportive means for social and community development. The STAR programme, aimed at the less developed areas of the EC, has been used to develop the telecommunications infrastructure for rural areas to stimulate the use of information networking for employment and skills development.

The ACE-HI scheme, administered by the Association of Community Enterprises in the Highland and Islands of Scotland is an example of this type of activity (with additional funding from BT), resulting in a £16 million investment in ISDN networks, and their successful use for the delivering of training and the development of enterprises which conduct their business through such networks, in remote islands and isolated parts of the mainland. Other EC social programmes have made extensive use of networking and telecommunications. The COMETT programme has used networking to promote trans-national co-operation between commercial enterprises and universities for the delivery of training in technical skills.

The HORIZON programme is establishing a disabled people's network through Europe, while the New Opportunities for Women programme is funding the partnership of Athens, Manchester, and Seville in building a telematics development network for the exchange of skills, information, and experience on women's training, employment, and enterprise.

The European Community established the ROME (Reseau Observatoires Metropolitains en Europe) network in 1989 to advise the Commission on research and information development activities for urban areas. A three-year project known as the European Urban Observatory was initiated in 1992 linking ten European cities (Amsterdam, Athens, Barcelona, Birmingham, Berlin, Genoa, Glasgow, Lille, Lisbon, and Naples) in a European-wide network to support strategic decision-making and the common interpretation of information on a European-wide basis. The aim of this project is to monitor urban trends through the sharing of urban management information, the transfer of experience and comparative evaluation of policy.

Information is structured into three levels, dealing with basic indicators for policy decision-making, with quantitative comparative data, and with individual city data stored locally; these levels are linked together through the use of X. 25 private networks, and the BT Tymnet wide area network employed to form a closed user group. This networking of public management information contributes to the development of pan-European urban policy issues, and gives a comparative background resource at the local level.

Information networking in the health service sector in the United Kingdom has become a vital activity in recent years, stimulated by a growing movement for the improvement of health information services, following the work of the Korner Group on information systems, and stimulated by the radical organizational changes creating an 'internal market' for purchasers and providers of health services. These tendencies have created a pressure for the harmonization and integration of all forms of information within the sector, and a demand for wider accessibility and sharing through computer networks and other applications of information technology.

The distinction between traditional bibliographic information services and other information sources has lessened with 'information' and 'intelligence' being taken to include, sometimes primarily, statistical and demographical information. Within this context, networks are used to link the office automation and service environment with information providers across many administrative levels.

Management information in this framework would include:

— literature in the form of written or audiovisual material: published books and journals, etc., as well as unpublished material in the form of correspondence, internal reports, and committee minutes;

— quantitative information, in the form of data relating to the activities and context of the organization; statistical returns, demographic analysis, performance indicators, trends analysis.

Within the health sector, an integrated delivery of information services more often requires sharing and exchange between fragmented units, now within a more competitive context. Library units, for example, may include within the same region headquarters libraries, departmental libraries, small service points in branch hospitals, postgraduate medical centre and research information points, and nursing libraries; each with varying degrees of autonomy.

With a growing amount of information available in electronic form, user requirements are likely to involve the retrieval of information from remote sources across a network, as much or more than from a local collection, and to varying forms and types of data. A medical researcher, for example, could require not only bibliographic references, and full text source material, but also images and the ability to process images, datasets of published social and epidemiological statistics, and so on. At the international level, medical information services are developing strengthened links through the use of networks.

The HealthNet system, for example, provides access for health professionals in developing countries to medical literature and databases and to colleagues elsewhere, through the use of low-cost packet satellite technology. HealthNet is initially targeted at Africa, and includes access to British and North American gateways which allow medical libraries and information units in these areas to 'twin' with similar organizations in Africa.

Generic facilities such as electronic mail and file transfer through computer networks open up the possibility of more extensive contact between health professionals in the context of an electronic community.

The increasing depth of special knowledge possessed by a widening spectrum of health professionals, located geographically separate from each other, and the interdisciplinary nature of health science, point towards a need for networked and integrated solutions to information needs. At the same time as information management has assumed a higher profile within the health sector, there is a growing interaction with external agencies fuelled by information interchange. Some instances of co-operative networking with local authorities have been mentioned earlier—a common interest in demographic analysis for strategic planning is another obvious example—and the same trend emerges in health service relations with other public service organizations.

The range and volume of data involved can be quite significant: a medium-sized hospital can send some 300-400 pathology and radiology reports per day to several dozen local general practitioner centres, and up to 100 discharge letters; a large general medical practice may make some 40 referrals per day to hospitals, and perhaps 7000 registrations per year to Family Health Service Authorities. Each of these activities involves the transmission of information and storage within the receiving systems, with the desirability of enabling the direct capture by the receiving application, and avoiding a need to re-key data which is already in electronic format.

The data needs to be exchanged between autonomous sites, loosely coupled in systems with a local focus. Externally, information flows will move from the National Health Service to product suppliers, service providers, government agencies, local authorities,

European and international organizations, the insurance and banking sectors, private health care agencies, and other national health services. To achieve an electronic data integration across the whole health service delivery chain, and with organizations in its environment, the development and application of standard forms of information interchange is required.

The United Nations standard for electronic data interchange EDIFACT has been adopted by the Information Management Executive of the UK National Health Service as a widely used and comprehensible standard. The EDIFACT standard requires the use of structured information formats primarily intended for autonomous computer processing, and transferral across telecommunication links.

The standard provides for the definition of data elements, syntax rules, and the structure of messages built from these data elements in a way that can be adapted for various applications; EDIFACT is managed by the United Nations as a cross-sector global communications standard, and is also defined within GOSIP, the UK Government Open System Profile. The NHS Information Management Executive has initiated many projects intended to contribute towards the development of a common infrastructure through the use of information systems strategy.

A major plank within this strategy is the desire to create a unique NHS number for individual patients, enabling the creation of a population register designed for sharing across the sector, and forming a natural integration of basic administrative activities. This will underpin NHS-wide electronic networking, and together with agreed standards for information interchange, lead towards a shared language for health care throughout the sector.

A number of these projects are aimed at general practitioners, and their links with other health agencies, involving the identification of a basic information structure common to all GP practices, and the development of compatible systems. Some examples of these development initiatives are:

— the electronic linking of GPs to hospitals for the exchange of pathology and waiting list information via the RACAL Healthlink system and local regional networks, in the Oxford Region GP/Hospital Information Exchange Project;

— linking general practitioners with Family Health Service authorities (FHSA) to enable the direct registration and update of FHSA databases by local practices, and vice versa, and the linked updating of payments to doctors through FHSA systems;

— the update of FHSA databases to the NHS Central Register (NHSCR) as the most reliable measure of movement of the population between Health Authority areas;

— an information collection project to network GPs together to facilitate the continuous collection of morbidity data as the basis for a national agreed set of morbidity data.

More broadly, projects are developing standards which apply across the sector, for:

— the development of a common basic specification as an extension of the NHS Data Model, to cover data exchange standards, minimum datasets, clinical information for resource management; and the information demands of hospital and regional decision support systems;

— the development of an NHS Administrative Register

to act as a shared register of basic administrative details meeting the requirements of District Health authorities, Family Health Service authorities, general practitioners, and hospitals;

— a Community Information Systems Project to facilitate the exchange of information to support contracting, and the development of datasets for ambulatory care in hospital and community settings, for use by community health services.

The National Health Service in the United Kingdom has seen a vast increase in the importance of information management, with information networking forming a vital part of this. It is certain that the importance of networking activities will continue to grow as a strategic element in the construction of integrated information and intelligence.

8

Maintain an Effective Service

There are several ways of monitoring a service, each with varying degrees of complexity. The method(s) you choose will depend on the amount of staff time and resources you have available. They are the following:

— statistics;

— feedback;

— surveys;

— research.

Statistics

There are very few people who would claim to like keeping statistics. At best, they are looked on as an irksome necessity, only tolerable when kept as unobtrusive as possible. Staff running a busy community information service will seldom have the time to keep detailed records of enquiries, so do try to restrict them to the absolute minimum. The barest minimum is simply to record the number of people using the centre by noting them down on a sheet of paper, using the time-honoured 'five barred gate' method or a number tally machine or 'clicker'. Both these methods rely on a human agent, however, and are therefore prone to inaccuracies—through forgetfulness, preoccupation, distraction, etc.

There are now counting devices, available which are triggered off by customers treading on a pressure pad placed under a carpet or by breaking an infra-red beam. This statistic will only tell you the number of people who darkened your doorstep, however; they might only have been browsing or sheltering from the rain, so an alternative is to record manually the number of people making an enquiry.

Nonetheless, you will not know what subjects they enquired about, whether you were successful in finding the information, or how long it took. You can go some way towards collecting more detail and yet not create much more work by drawing up or pre-printing record sheets. These may be related to subject or length of time or both. Some centres, instead of using sheets, have a bank of 'clickers', but this is only practicable if you have a small number of categories, say no more than six; otherwise it becomes too complicated to remember which 'clicker' is which. All the above methods give only a broad indication of the number of enquiries and do not reveal any detail about their nature or the degree of success in answering them.

The latter aspect might be catered for by asking staff to record details of unsuccessful enquiries only, so that they can be analysed in order to detect any weaknesses in the information base that can be rectified or any sources that have been overlooked. A more detailed recording system, found mainly in advice and counselling centres, is the day book. In effect, this is a large diary in which details of enquiries are recorded, giving the name of the client, address, date and nature of the enquiry, action taken, further action being pursued, etc. A day book has the advantage of being easy to use and allows other information and advice workers to check on the details of an enquiry if the person calls back on another occasion. It is not so convenient for extracting statistics and, should you need to refer back to an enquiry, the chronological arrangement is not helpful—people can be notoriously vague about dates. A more satisfactory method is to enter the details on cards or pre-printed enquiry forms, one for each client. These can then be filed by the client's name, so that it is easy to refer back if some time has elapsed between visits.

The system of pre-printed enquiry forms is fairly common in information centres but is rarely used for all enquiries—usually only those that take some time or require further search after the enquirer has left the centre or hung up the phone. The kinds of information that you may want to collect about each enquiry can include the following:

— *Client*—name, address, telephone number (if needed for follow-up), sex, Age range, ethnic origin.
— *Enquiry— simple* precis of subject.
— *Duration*—how long it took to answer the enquiry.
— *Sources used or tried in answering the enquiry—useful* if a search is continued over a length of time to avoid duplication of effort.
— *How enquiry was received—walk-in,* telephone, post, fax.
— *Time—will* indicate spread of enquiries throughout the day.
— *How client heard* of *service—may* help to measure success of publicity.
— *Client's area* of *residence* (if address not taken)—will show from which areas most use comes and those not being reached.

Forms have the advantage that they can easily be stored for future reference and abstracting of statistics. With a subject heading or classification number added, they can become a subject file to be referred to when information on the same subject or statistics are required. In a very busy information centre, however, it is unlikely that staff will have time to fill in a form with this amount of detail for each enquiry, so you may need to consider a combination of (a) forms for lengthier enquiries and those needing to be followed up, and (b) a tally system under broad categories for quick enquiries.

The record sheet shown here is a kind of compromise hybrid that was used for recording enquiries in a public library community information centre shared with other agencies on a sessional basis. Each agency had its own pad of forms which were self-carbonated to produce an additional copy for the librarian to extract statistics. If you have invested in a computer, there is the temptation to use it for collecting statistics. After all, computers are eminently suited to number crunching, particularly if you need to ask detailed question of your enquiry statistics, such as 'How many women aged over sixty living in the Westward area of Exville enquired about bus passes in 1991?' Where you are simply keeping a tally of the number of enquiries in a number of broad categories, then it is debatable whether a computer will save you much time. Before you start using a computer to store statistics, make sure that you have an effective system for recording enquiries in the first place; otherwise the old computer adage of 'garbage in, garbage out' will apply.

London Advice Services Alliance is currently working on a model system for recording statistics for advice work, called STATS. There are four aspects to STATS: a Classification System, Sample Recording Forms, Guidance and Training. The project will take several years to complete and for more details and progress, contact LASA at 88-94 Wentworth Street, London E1 7SA.

Feedback

Statistics can tell you how many people used your information service, how many enquiries they made, when and on what subjects, but they will not reveal whether users are satisfied with the service or why others do not use your service. To get some idea of the impact your service is making on its community, you need to have a means of getting feedback from that community. Two ways of doing this have already been referred to elsewhere in this book.

One of the functions of the management committee was identified as to 'monitor use and recommend changes'. If, as suggested, this committee includes representatives of the community, then their comments will be very important in assessing how well the service is: doing. It was suggested that a spin-off from publicizing a service by means of talks to community groups was that it also gave an opportunity for the speaker to ask for reactions to the service and discover any needs not being met. There is a practice, associated mainly with information and referral (I&R) centres in the United States, called 'follow-up', which is used to check on user satisfaction with the service or services to which they have been referred. At the time of the enquiry, details of the client's name and telephone number, the query and the service(s) to which referred are noted down. Then, at a later date, the client is rung back to find out if the information given was satisfactory or whether further help is required.

Any adverse comments about the I&R centre are noted, so that improvements can be made. Comments about other services are noted down on the back of the appropriate card for that service in the information file. In this way, clients are encouraged to feel that they are a part of the information service and can contribute to the continual evaluation of its information files. However, follow-up is a time-consuming and costly exercise which may well be beyond the means of most community information services except on an occasional and very selective basis.

You may be able to get some useful feedback by consulting other information and advice services or community leaders in your area. They may have had comments made to them about your service and be prepared to divulge them with frankness.

Surveys

A more formal and systematic way to obtain feedback is to conduct a user survey or a general survey of your community. You do not have to be an experienced researcher to carry out a survey, provided you exercise a degree of commonsense and care in drafting or asking questions. Before you conduct a survey, you must have a clear idea of what you want to find out and the use to which that information is going to be put. You may only want to gather information about the existing clientele of your service, in which case a user survey is called for.

On the other hand, it may be important to find out what impact your service is making on the community as a whole; therefore, the scope of the survey needs to be wider and to be conducted outside the information centre. There are basically two methods of conducting a survey, by questionnaire and by interview. A questionnaire survey of users is the easiest to carry out as, once the form has been drafted and printed, there is little staff involvement until the analysis stage. Questionnaires can be either left on the counter for clients to take or handed to clients when an enquiry is made. The following are points to look out for:

— Number forms so that you know how many have

been issued and can calculate the percentage returned.

— Make sure there is an address for returning the form and a closing date—you do not necessarily have to keep to the closing date but it helps to encourage people to return them.

— Have an open question on the form to invite any other comments about the service—this often evokes the best replies.

— Arrange a system for return of forms that has a degree of anonymity (e.g. a posting box in the centre).

With this kind of survey, it is usual to find that responses tend to be biased towards the favourable, so you will have to allow for this when interpreting results. The other method of surveying users is by interview. This has the advantages that it is possible for the interviewer to probe for greater depth in responses, to record qualified replies to questions where the interviewee has difficulty in giving a straight yes/no response, and the interviewee can ask for clarification of any questions on which they are not sure.

A disadvantage of this method, of course, is that the more non-standardized the replies, the more difficult they are to analyse and represent statistically. You will need space in your centre to conduct interviews and staff time, although it may be possible to enlist outside help with this in the shape of volunteers or students on placement. It is unlikely that you will be able to interview every user, so an agreed proportion must be determined beforehand, say every other one or every tenth. Whatever the proportion, you will probably need two interviewers, as it is not possible for one person to interview and keep an eye on the numbers using the service in order to catch the next one. With more than one interviewer it becomes necessary to ensure that questions are posed in the same way, especially when there is a need to prompt interviewees, and that means some form of training or briefing beforehand. The remarks above about allowing for favourable bias in interpreting replies also applies here, possibly to an even greater extent, since clients are unlikely to be outwardly critical of a service when being interviewed on its premises.

A survey of the wider community needs to be drafted more carefully. Where possible, try to disguise the purpose of the survey and avoid asking leading questions ('Don't you think it's a good idea to . . .') as these may colour responses. It is unlikely with both questionnaires and interviews that you will be aiming for total coverage of the community, so decide on a representative sample. There are several possible ways of distributing questionnaires, the least satisfactory being to leave copies in public buildings (community centres, libraries, council offices, shops, clinics, etc.) for people to take. This is somewhat haphazard and may not result in a representative sample.

A better alternative is to deliver by hand to every tenth house (or whatever proportion you have decided), using your own staff or volunteers. There may, however, be a simpler way of distributing by, for example, inserting copies in the appropriate proportion of community newspapers (where they exist) that are delivered to each household. You might investigate the possibility of printing the survey as part of the community newspaper. Where you can afford it, include a post-paid, addressed envelope for reply; otherwise, arrange for them to be left at suitable locations in the community.

Interviewing of the wider community to determine use is unlikely to be a practical proposition for an information centre to conduct on its own. It is more likely to be used where an outside organization is conducting a research project on your service.

Research

Surveys are one form of research, of which there are a number of other types—operational research, action research, experimental research - most of which require a certain amount of expertise and, therefore, will need to be conducted by an outside agency, e.g. The British Library, a library school, or a university department. Interest in your information service as a subject of research will depend on whether it has innovative features or whether the aspect to be investigated is symptomatic of other information centres and thus the research findings would have a wide applicability.

Continuous evaluation using one or several of the techniques outlined above is essential in order to keep the service relevant to its community. By indicating strengths and weaknesses, areas of unmet need and duplication of services, it can point the way to future development of the information service. An information service needs to be a growing organism because communities do not stand still but are constantly changing, some more rapidly than others. At the beginning of this book, we stressed the need to involve the community in the planning of your information service and that is my message at the end.

A community information service exists to serve its community and, therefore, the community needs to be involved at all stages. There is no guarantee, in these hard times, that your service will survive, but it stands a much better chance of succeeding and developing if it can be shown that it is respected, valued and used by the community and is performing a worthwhile function.

9

Development of Telecommunications

In the past, telecommunications has largely been regarded as a natural monopoly in the same way as gas and electricity. The long-term nature of the investment needed to create a national infrastructure, and the massive amounts of capital involved, have discouraged private initiative and relied upon governmental support and backing.

During the 1980s, in many countries around the world, this arrangement began to be perceived as too parochial and inflexible; liberalization of tele-communications regulation was seen as a means of stimulating innovation, by encouraging the development of market forces through the introduction of new service suppliers.

The liberalization of telecommunication has taken two main forms. they are the following:

— *Privatization*: In which the monopoly authority is established as a private corporation, which competes on the same terms as any other business;

— *Deregulation*: In which allows new service operators to offer competitive services, by the removal of restrictive practices which legislate against this.

Many countries have opted for a mixture of these two forms, often with a transition period setting special conditions which alternative services must adhere to. The extent of deregulation has also differed considerably; since the telecommunications infrastructure is seen as so essential to economic development, the total abolition of all regulatory mechanisms is not considered desirable. For this reason, many people speak of re-regulation, stressing a change in the conditions of government control rather than their complete removal.

The United States has historically been different from most countries, in that telecommunications have always been controlled by a private corporation, licensed under government monopoly. The AT&T corporation which provided the telephone systems prior to liberalization was forbidden in a 1956 ruling from entering the computer or information business, in which it would be considered to have an unfair advantage. In this period, two major corporations, AT&T and IBM, dominated the telecommunications and computing industries respectively, but did not directly compete with each other. A Federal Court ruling of 1982 ended this arrangement by requiring the divestiture of AT&T under the corporate anti-trust laws. This resulted in the creation of seven independent regional Bell operating companies out of the former AT&T conglomerate, each of which provided the public telecommunications service in a separate geographical area of the United States.

AT&T itself remained to compete for the traffic between these regions with other long haul private network operators, such as MCI and US Sprint. AT&T was also permitted to enter the computer and information business in its own right which, as the original developer and licensor of the Unix operating system through Bell Laboratories, was an attractive new direction for its corporate development. This 1982 judgment did not, however, end all regulation over the sector. The divested AT&T was prevented from entering 'electronic publishing'—the provision of information services on their networks—for a period of seven years while competitor network suppliers developed their strengths. This restriction was removed in 1989. The regional Bell operating companies (RBOCs) are now permitted to offer:

— electronic messaging;

— audiotex;

— electronic gateways to other information services;

— integrated billing for online information through these gateways;

The AT&T corporation, however, acting as the carrier of inter-exchange traffic, is increasingly interested in developing information services through co-operation with the regional operating companies; for example by using national customer databases of names and addresses for credit card and target marketing schemes.

The exact relationship between monopoly and non-monopoly services has been the subject of debate and conflict between the Federal Court and the Federal Communications Commission throughout this period, with the former championing a more restrictive approach. Realizing that the computer industry which telecommunications serves has global interests, both AT&T and the RBOCs are also diversifying into foreign markets, both as telecommunications carriers and as providers of online services, following the creation of new opportunities through liberalization abroad. Although the trend has had an uneven develo-pment, there has been a steady blurring of the distinction between information provider, information vendor, and telecommunications carrier which will continue in the present decade.

The same global trends have affected the structure and development of the telecommunications and information industries in Europe, but here the influence of the large multinational corporations has been diluted by a more robust government policy concerned to afford some protection to national and regional interests.

Within the European Community (EC) public data networks evolved independently in separate countries, resulting in a smaller overall market for each and a relatively higher cost of equipment than in the United States. This concentration on a national scope has led to the development of somewhat different technology, in particular the installation of different digital switching systems, which reduces the potential for European connectivity as a whole. The European Commission has taken an active interest in the development of the telecommunications facilities within the member countries, where the role of the PTTs has been crucial in the growth from fledgling services to sophisticated international networking. A major project sponsored by the EC which helped to fuel this growth was the Euronet service developed in the late 1970s.

The EC commissioned the national PTTs to create a packet switching network capable of supporting access from all the member countries, and itself mounted a variety of information services on the network under its own auspices as well as encouraging the development of others. This initiative gave a boost to the developing information industries in Europe, helping to create a market sector in which information vendors could establish themselves, while the PTTs were engaged in building up their own national packet switching networks to an adequate standard for a reliable international service. Once these had begun operation, Euronet was discontinued in 1984. This period saw the development of Packet SwitchStream in the United

Kingdom, and similar ventures in France, the Netherlands, and Germany. These developments were driven through at the national level, with little detailed co-ordination between network suppliers who increasingly came to view each other as business competitors. This has resulted in the duplication of services and multiple international links to the United States and the Far East, with the network suppliers effectively competing to capture the market for data traffic entering and leaving Europe. The European Commission has been concerned to develop international research and development programmes, and has used the liberalization programme to stimulate innovation and corporate investment, in order to build a compatible European communication infrastructure capable of supporting the open internal market from 1993.

The creation of a European Telecommunications Standards Institute and the progressive reform of the PTT authorities have been explicit actions taken to support the declared EC objectives of:

— opening all network services, except the basic phone and data transmission services, to full competition;

— opening the terminal market to competition, within accepted operating standards;

— establishing uniform telecommunications charging across the EC;

— creating European standards for equipment to increase compatibility and remove trade barriers.

To support research and development, the Commission has embarked on programmes intended to develop the economic power of the region through advanced telecommunications technology. The RACE programme is a ten year effort, begun in 1985, to develop the standards and technology for integrated broadband communication through EC funded project teams drawn from industry and the academic world. The less favoured regions of the EC are supported by the STAR programme, which funds in part the development costs of upgrading communications infrastructures in the more rural areas of Greece, Ireland, Portugal, Spain, France and the United Kingdom.

The development of narrowband ISDN, however, has not progressed as fast as considered desirable by the EC, which set itself a target of 5% market penetration by 1993 a decade earlier; in early 1992 there were only five commercial ISDN networks in operation in the EC and it was forecast that only 1% would be achieved, failing to impact small and medium sized enterprises and the residential sector. This slow progress is due to a lack of standardization in ISDN technology, a consequent lack of cheap equipment available for the mass market, and an unwillingness on the part of network operators to take committed action in the face of this uncertainty. Within the EC, individual countries have taken a path of deregulation; rather than of complete privatization. Many former publicly owned PTTs have been transformed into private companies, but often with a majority shareholding still held by the State; and although these compete with private corporations in some areas, most still retain a degree of monopolistic privilege and control which in some cases can be quite substantial.

In the United Kingdom, changes in telecommunications occurred within a more general perspective of a Conservative government free-market philosophy committed to reversal of state monopoly industries in general. The successive Telecommunications Acts of 1981 and 1984 separated telecommunications from the postal authority, establishing British Telecom (now BT) as a private corporation.

At the same time, licences to offer similar services were granted to other companies, with the intention of creating a competitive market which would encourage innovation and efficiency. The principal competitor was Mercury Communications, founded for this purpose by Cable and Wireless; two other licences have also been granted for the establishment of cellular radiophone services. A curiosity of the British situation was the third licensed operator, the city of Kingston upon Hull, which for historical reasons already ran its own local phone system; so successfully, that it was able to provide free local phone calls. This was privatized in 1987 as Kingston Communications, eventually becoming part of a larger corporation. The 1984 Act also created OfTel, the Office of Telecommunications, charged with administering the regulatory structure and overseeing the implementation of the licensing conditions imposed on operators, to protect the public interest and ensure fair trading. These included, for instance, a requirement for Mercury to develop a commitment to geographical coverage of the United Kingdom as well as more specialist business services.

Mercury Communications was originally targeted at large corporations, but since obtaining the right to interconnect with the BT network, and thenceforth the ability to provide complete end-to-end services has extended beyond its limited geographic base to provide data services to medium and smaller businesses. As well as digital phone services, Mercury now provides a packet switched data network under the name of Mercury 5000, and an ISDN service called Premier 2100. In this way, it is now competing with BT in all major areas, and is actively co-operating with foreign companies such as AT&T to provide advanced satellite network services. While Mercury has built an all-digital network from the start but has limited geographic coverage, BT has a completely national service but is only just becoming fully digital in operation. At the same time as upgrading its national network, however, BT has developed international networking capabilities, for instance by the acquisition of the US-based value added network Tymnet, and has developed a range of value added services for delivery on these networks. There are two levels of integrated digital services, ISDN-2 and ISDN-30, with connections to ISDN networks in many other countries. In conjunction with this, BT provides videoconferencing and 'narrowcast' television services for intra-corporate communications. There is no restriction in the UK on the development of information services by the carrier operators, and BT in particular has developed many such services. The Prestel system was an early venture in videotex or viewdata, but has had little long lasting success despite being one of the first examples in this field.

Although successful in niche areas such as travel and insurance, after ten years of operation Prestel had only 95,000 terminals in use, and had failed to fulfil its original objectives of serving a mainly residential domestic market. Business oriented information services have proved more successful in areas such as financial, currency, market, and company information. Despite deriving some benefit from a loose regulatory structure which in practice has shielded BT from some of the effects of direct competition, the lack of a unifying structure under which services are offered, and a general philosophy of 'let the market decide' has retarded the development of a strong direction for telecommunications in the UK.

The relatively low cost of leased lines, for example, favours the building of private networks and encourages third-party suppliers of value added services, while discouraging the take-up of national services such as

ISDN. BT must therefore compete on the same terms as these third party suppliers, and increasingly on an international basis. A further round of liberalization has opened up the possibility of other interested organisations applying for a licence to offer telecommunications services. These potentially may include:

— cable TV franchises, which have extensive links to customer premises, but no national infrastructure,

— cellular phone services, which are now allowed to build trunk networks, and could offer a packet switched radio-based network;

— recently de-regulated satellite services, able to both receive and transmit from small and cheap terminal devices;

— other national industries, such as British Rail, which have extensive rights of way for laying cable.

The cost of entering the telecommunications market in a competitive age is likely to mean that any of these options would be likely to seek an alliance with a foreign network provider, with particular interest expressed from United States Bell companies.

The relationship between the telecommunications authority and the State has been markedly different in France. The national PTT was established as France Telecom in 1986, a private corporation owned by the State. The organisation largely retained control over equipment approvals policy and operating conditions, able, for instance, to levy a 30% surcharge on leased lines used for value added services by competitors and to prevent certain kinds of services altogether. The Transpac X.25 public packet switching network is claimed to be the largest in the world, and has extended its value added services across Europe, including the recent acquisition of the London Regional Transport network in the United

Kingdom. Transpac is already used by some United Kingdom companies for facilities such as electronic data interchange, in preference to leased lines from BT or Mercury, and is expected to be a major competitor in the European open market for telecommunications services.

The best known success of the French PTT has been the Minitel service. This videotex service, in contrast to the British Prestel, is now the dominant videotex system in Europe and has been sold to many other network operators, including NTT in Japan, the Italian PTT, and the Bell company US West.

From its first operation in 1983, Minitel grew to 4 million connected terminals in its first five years, and nearly 6 million in 1992, of which at least half are business users. Videotex is generally seen as providing access to large databases of information, presented through an easy to use interface which is accessible without special knowledge or instruction.

The system was originally developed by telecommunications interests as a suitable information service for linking the telephone with a domestic television set, but is now often supplemented by an intelligent terminal or personal computer.

A major reason for the initial success of Minitel lay in the policy of freely loaning the specially designed Minitel terminals to telephone subscribers, at the same time as replacing the printed telephone directory with an electronic version accessible only by videotex.

The Electronic Directory, provides access to a national database of phone subscribers through a simple enquiry language, as well as Yellow Pages information. The great success of this service very quickly created a substantial user base for Minitel, which encouraged other information suppliers to participate by offering other information services. These other services now cover a wide range, aimed at both the business and domestic markets, and including:

1. Electronic messaging; professional services; business and financial information; domestic shopping and banking services; and chat lines.
2. The Pancatalogue comprising the online catalogue of the Bibliotheque Nationale and of the SIBIL user group of 22 universities is accessible via Minitel; the new French national library, due to open in 1995, plans a Minitel link which will enable the user to reserve materials from home, and book a reading place for a particular arrival time,
3. Newspaper publishers offer a package of services including news bulletins; information on sport, entertainment and leisure; classified advertisements and games.
4. Professional level services include access to a range of online databases with sophisticated search interfaces. Services are organized in a kiosque system, in which the user has the available services displayed, but pays only for actual use with no fixed subscription fee. There are seven different levels of charging for information used, priced per hour of usage regardless of distance, ranging from almost nominal fees to typical online database searching rates. The vendor is responsible for mounting the information, and chooses the applicable charging rate. Teletel, the service umbrella under which Minitel is managed, provides access through the Transpac network, and includes the user charge in the normal telephone bill on behalf of the vendor. An international service is being introduced which interlinks with other national videotex services, and with Teletel hosts abroad.

France Telecom opened its Numeris ISDN network in Brittany in 1987, and established a national network by 1990. The development of suitable applications was encouraged by a partnership scheme in which France Telecom sponsored pilot projects with commercial and client organisations, paying half of the research and development costs.

Many of these applications involved the transmission of high definition images, such as the transfer of X-ray and ultra-sound images between medical sites in emergency cases, the transmission of satellite weather images, and the distribution of high definition house pictures around a network-of estate agents.

In Germany the PTT authority was turned into a private corporation, owned by the State, in 1989. Prior to this, the Deutsches Bundespost had resisted the encroachment of competitor services by keeping prices high for leased lines, charging by volume rather than by fixed rental, and by refusing equipment approval.

The 1989 reform following re-unification created a Bundespost subsidiary Telekom, and allowed private companies to compete in establishing value added services, although it has been reluctant to change this policy. The Deutsches Bundespost established a basic rate ISDN in eight major German cities in 1989, and expanded this to a broader national network, using the promotion of applications as a development device in a more limited way than the French experience. Telekom currently offers the following services:

— a videotex system, called BTX, similar to Prestel;

— an electronic mail system, called Telebox;

— a facility for remote monitoring of industrial plant and processes.

The development of the telecommunications infrastructure has stimulated the growth of the information industry, creating a larger potential market for information suppliers by bringing many more people into the communications web, building a more reliable and higher quality service.

The European informatics organisation, Eusidic, organizes an annual monitoring exercise on the reliability of international packet switching services by asking its members to record a typical week of use. This has recorded a steady increase in reliability, showing a 25% failure rate in calls in 1988 compared with a 14% failure rate in 1991; a large proportion of these faults are believed to occur when a dial-up connection through the PSTN telephone line is used as a local link to the packet switching exchange. An increase in, the total number of packet, switching exchanges in many European countries has reduced the importance of this link, and simplified the installation of new network connections. More dependable communications together with a network infrastructure which is capable of offering a connection to all potential customers has led to a substantial growth in the number of databases produced in both Europe and the United States, and in the number of host systems which offer access to them.

By 1990, there were estimated to be 1048 databases produced in EC countries and 2214 produced in the United States, excluding those only available in videotex model; this represented an 11% growth rate per annum in EC countries and a 7% growth rate in the United States. Within the EC the same report counted 227 hosts offering access to a total of 1256 databases, and 299 online hosts giving access to 3348 databases in the United States, although this is counting some databases more than once when they are accessible from several different hosts.

Compared with earlier surveys, this figure indicates that the number of hosts in Europe is growing while those in the United States are remaining stable. A similar growth has taken place in the professional and business database usage sector of the videotex market in Europe, although the trends here are not so marked.

The French Minitel system dominates the area, with just over 85% of the total number of installed terminals across Europe (6.6 million) in that country; some 50% of the estimated 5 million or so Minitel customers are professional users compared to about 80% of the 100,000 Prestel users in the United Kingdom.

Overall the European Commission estimated that there were 15,000 information providers on European videotex in 19912, although once again most of these are mounted on the Minitel system which provides the predominant means of access to professional information services in France.

The distribution of the online market is uneven, with the United Kingdom, France, and Germany accounting for about 70% of the market share, the majority of which is held by the United Kingdom. The large number of potential databases, of which many can often be consulted through competing hosts at varying charging rates and using different command languages as the search interface, is a source of confusion and uncertainty for the end-user.

The diversity of choice has led to a growth in the use of gateways, links through from one system to another. Gateways in telecommunications networks can take one of three main forms:

1. Conversion facilities which link dissimilar systems and information types by translating back and forth between the two, typically used for the forwarding of electronic mail between systems.

2. Hosts which have a link through to other relevant hosts in their own area of interest, so that the second can be contacted directly through the first: the user can drop out to the second host, consult the services available, and then return to the first host on completion.
3. Value added services, which provide a 'front end' to a range of databases on different hosts, to ease and enhance user access by masking detailed differences between hosts in a common presentation and interface.

The use of value added networks has been an established part of the online scene for many years, especially attractive in situations where the reliability of the public telecommunications network cannot be guaranteed. The Dialnet value added network used by Dialog Information Services is an example. This offers regular users a local network connection point with billing for telecommunications costs integrated with that for database usage, as an alternative to dealing separately with international telecommunications vendors.

A third-party gateway service takes this a step further by offering integrated access to many different hosts through one connection.

A well-known example is the Easynet service, which allows users to access more than 900 databases on various hosts; the user may select a database directly or enter the relevant criteria for the service to select automatically the most appropriate one itself. The service offers one command language (the Common Command Language) to all the host systems made available, so that the user is not required to learn new search languages and unfamiliar systems are made more accessible. The Common Command Language reduces the degree of sophistication possible in search statements by imposing commonality, so there are facilities for the experienced user to express the search in the native host language. The Easynet gateway also provides management facilities for monitoring the most effective database usage, and for controlling the costs of use throughout the process. This growth in the online information market in both provision and usage is predicted to continue at increasing rates, with market research forecasts continually revised upwards.

The expanding availability of information services and the almost ubiquitous presence of telecommunications networks is beginning to have a substantial impact not only on the way in which traditional information consumers such as libraries and information units are conducting their activities, but also on the development of new information-related occupations which can take advantage of these new communications features.

The practice of teleworking—the conduct of work-related business and interactions over a distance and through the telecommunications networks: with the employer, with colleagues, with customers and contractors—is one of these areas.

The development of information networking, in both the informal and personal sense as well as a formal substitution of electronically-mediated work relations, is fundamental to the growth of distance working. A major plank, in the telecommunications development programme of the European Community has been the encouragement of teleworking through funding of the necessary infrastructure, as a means of economic development in rural and less-favoured regions of Europe. An example of this is the development initiative conducted in conjunction with BT to provide digital exchanges and line plant for the installation of integrated digital services in the Highlands and Islands region of Scotland in the Hi-ISDN project.

A complementary project, called Hi-VANS, provides an easy to use interface to national and international services and to the public data network, as well as local information services for the development of tourism and community enterprises. An example of one such enterprise is the use of the network to transmit scanned images of articles which require abstracting from the Elsevier journal publisher in the Netherlands to distance workers in the Highlands. The articles are scanned in the Netherlands from the print version and sent to abstracters in Scotland; the completed abstracts are then returned for publication to the Netherlands with no production delays arising from postal delivery times.

Similar pioneering efforts have seen the foundation of 'telecottages' in many rural areas of the United Kingdom. A 'telecottage' is a generic term for a rural information technology centre, which provides easy access to IT, usually in a public building and on an informal basis. The telecottage can provide formal and informal training, and can act as a catalyst for small enterprises by providing cost-effective access to equipment, as well as supporting the work of community groups.

Apart from public funding, this concept has found sponsorship in the United Kingdom from BT in the form of four Teleservice Centres, established as well-equipped telematic service centres; the first of these to begin activity was in the Shetland Islands in 1991. The willingness of a major telecommunications corporation to become so involved in stimulating the development of a networking infrastructure for information enterprises testifies to the potential possibilities for the future.

In Europe, the concept of teleworking was developed first in Scandinavia, spreading quickly to the United Kingdom, and is now strongly favoured by government and EC initiatives in France, Spain and Portugal. The Telecottage Association, formed to support the growth in teleworking through personal networks of groups and individuals by means of seminars and newsletters, estimates that there are about 590,000 self-employed teleworkers in the United Kingdom. Many of these people are professional workers to whom the production, use and exchange of information is vital to their work.

The recent acceptance of distance working indicates a trend towards more skilled information workers, and the replacement of traditional office work by advisory, and consultancy-based work which does not require full-time attendance at a particular geographical location to be carried out. This is demonstrated by the Telemedicine project in northern Norway, for example, which provides specialist medical services from a central hospital in Tromsoe to isolated local hospitals and health centres through the telecommunications network. This links together services such as pathology, radiology, and cardiology with access to medical databases and patient information systems for remote diagnosis, without requiring the patient to make a difficult journey to the central hospital facilities.

Generally, teleworking can take a number of different organisational forms:

- home-working, in which the workers are based at their own home, making few visits to an employer premises;
- telecentres, which offer new information technology facilities for workers from various different organisations;

— satellite work centres, which are owned by a large company but are geographically dispersed;

— flexible working, in which the work is carried out partly at the organisational premises and partly at home.

These new organisational forms imply changes in the overall structures for, organisational communications, and an increased emphasis on the development of networks which are capable of stretching beyond the physical confines of organisational premises alone.

Private network

The backbone of the private network is often provided by leased lines rented on the basis of sole use from the local telecommunications authority. The costs and conditions which are imposed on the lease differ quite widely between countries. Where lines are cheaper, as in the United Kingdom for example, a large corporation may now be able to justify a leased line on the basis of voice transmission only, using one Megastream line to replace several analogue phone lines, and be able to transmit data 'for free' on top of this usage since a fixed annual rent is paid. High bandwidth circuits such as these supply point to point connections, and are appropriate between sites which have a high data traffic flow. Dial-up lines may be used where small amounts of data are sent at infrequent intervals, possibly using parts of a public packet switched network.

Since 1989 organisations operating private networks are allowed to resell spare capacity on their bandwidth, so that linking in with an existing private network already in use elsewhere may be one option; for example, banks may make network capacity available to some of their corporate customers. While terrestrial lines are normally controlled by a telecommunications authority, since the liberalization of services nonterrestrial transmission offers a wider range of choices. Microwave links can be installed in line of sight between tall buildings, and satellite services can be employed to carry audio, video, and data services within a wide geographical area.

In the United States an 'open skies' policy, under which any qualified organisation can apply for a licence to operate a domestic satellite service, has been in operation since 1972; in the United Kingdom, however, the granting of full licences has been more reticent. Satellite capacity is available from a number of specialist data communications companies, and in Europe through the Eutelsat consortium of PTT authorities.

The pricing for Eutelsat usage is differentiated by member country with wide discrepancies in national rates; recently, clients have been able to book capacity through any member offering the best service. The development of very small aperture satellite transmission (VSAT) has lowered the relative costs of this medium, since a receive-only dish uses the same technology as satellite television, and can be installed with the same case without the need for formal planning permission. This can provide a low cost 'point-to-multi-point' data broadcasting, for fast updating of many sites simultaneously; and is also used as a stop-gap measure for establishing a network link quickly, or to link sites which are separated by difficult geographic terrain.

Cellular network radiophones can also be used for non-terrestrial data links, but are not yet ideal for this purpose. This method appears attractive for linking a portable personal computer fitted with integral modem into a corporate network from uncertain locations; however, the cellular channel is noisy, and the transition between cells introduces delays in which contact may easily be lost, preventing truly mobile data communications. Although the transmission of packet data over the VHF radio waveband is feasible, its widespread use has not yet developed in the United Kingdom; licences have only been granted to radio data companies for quite limited and specialized markets. The wide area networking elements also take on an international dimension if the organisation needs to link into sites in other countries.

Larger organisations have diverse information needs, and sometimes specialist but vital performance requirements, demanding the development of a networking strategy which is flexible and controllable. For information networking to support corporate communications, the organisation has three main choices.

1. To build a private network, using network elements from different sources.

2. To send data over one or other of the public data networks.

3. To hand over all network management aspects to a third party specializing in this field.

These choices have varying significance for different sizes and types of organisation operating in different fields; these disparate demands will lead to differing perceptions of the technology which is at the leading edge for a particular situation.

Smaller organisations, or those in which the information and technological infrastructure is less developed, may be well satisfied with options which are already considered obsolete by those in which information has a high strategic or mission importance. The use of public telecommunications in one organisation may have as far-reaching effects within that context, as are sought by another which is planning frame relay and broadband networking as replacements for X.25 and ISDN.

Some significant advantages of the use of public data services are given below:

1. The development of private networks demands the use of scarce personnel with technical expertise in networking skills, and a high capital investment; while using public networks leaves the organisation free to concentrate on its main activities without draining off resources.

2. Once a private network is developed it is hard to change, and expensive to upgrade with technological advances. Information activities may demand a high capacity at critical times, but may not justify this permanently (for example, with seasonal peaks in retail transactions); variable use of the public data network will smooth out peaks and troughs of this nature.

3. The broader scope of public services can develop targeted services for particular needs in a cost effective way, and save on the duplication of effort.

4. In a similar way, organisations can take advantage of the emergence of international standards through participation in a more general service, without the cost of individual development; for example, electronic data interchange standards for basic business documents.

The use of completely private networks, can have important attractions especially to a larger organisation which is able to amortise costs over a longer period.

1. The strategic importance of information to the organisation may demand control over the data at all stages, without fear of compromising security and confidentiality.

2. Control of the network enables technological decisions on speed and efficiency, the use of proprietary protocols, and flexible changes in response to need.
3. Control also extends to economic factors, where the unpredictable nature of changes in public services are avoided while spare capacity can be resold to other clients.

The third choice available to organisations is the use of third-party services to take over the management of all network facilities on its behalf. This removes the need for specialist expertise and keeps the technology up to date, while retaining some control and security, by making this the responsibility of an expert networking company. This is an attractive option to a medium sized organisation where communications is important for its business-but not of vital strategic importance-particularly if this involves the use of international connections and the consequent complexity of dealing with different national authorities. Network management companies may offer project management in the development of a network for a specific problem within a defined budget, or full *facilities management* of all networking arrangements.

Liberalization of telecommunications has encouraged the growth of management services from both private companies and the telecommunications carriers, while the increasing complexity of networking has made their services attractive to the client. The operators have often evolved from organisations which have established their own extensive private networks.

10

Artificial Intelligence and the Fifth Generation

Yet the current supercomputers are only at the threshold of what computer designers think can be achieved; the next generation of advanced supercomputers will make today's machines look like handheld calculators. "We have problems that would take 500 to 1,000 hours to solve [on today's supercomputers]," says David Nowak, division leader for computational physics at Lawrence Livermore National Laboratory, where a cluster of seven supercomputers-known as "Octopus"—is used for nuclear weapons research.

Before the end of the century, computer scientists hope to develop machines that not only crunch numbers at high speed but also exhibit artificial intelligence—computers that can think and reason somewhat like human beings and that can understand information conveyed by sight, speech, and motion. The question is, which nation's scientists will get there first? The Japanese have announced a two-pronged plan to build advanced computer technologies.

One project is the $100 million, eight-year National

Superspeed Computer project, which aims at producing machines 1000 times faster than the existing Cray-1 supercomputer built by Cray Research of Minneapolis. The other, the $500 million, 10-year Fifth Generation Computer project, is focussing on artificial intelligence. Both are now being countered by American efforts, including a Pentagon request for up to $1 billion over the next five years for superspeed and artificial intelligence (AI) technologies. Although behind, Great Britain and France have also launched national supercomputer projects. The great danger for the losers in the race-and the opportunity for the winners-is that whoever builds the next generation of computers will have a huge technological and commercial advantage: these computers win be used for computer and microelectronics design-to build even smarter, and more powerful machines. They won't be self-replicating machines, but they will be close. "It takes you a long time to catch up," says computer scientist Rai Reddy of Carnegie-Mellon University, one of the top us computer-research centers. "In some of these areas, that is the difference between a first-rate power and a second-rate power-from an economic point of view and from a security point of view. " The losers in the race will fall farther and farther behind. The leading edge of computer science is still a black art; there are no fixed laws, and the field is highly experimental. That is what worries us scientists about Japan's approach-some success is inevitable. "Because the field is experimental, [the Japanese] will come out with something," says Dertouzos. "It may not be what they wanted, but they'll come up with new architectures, new insights, -new design techniques.

To build the computers that will dominate the 1990s, both Japan and the us are depending on the onrushing technological advances in microelectronics. Japan's Fifth Generation project will use faster, denser circuitry to create a new class of superintelligent computers.

The 24 projects in the Fifth Generation concentrate on artificial intelligence, a goal of American computer scientists for more than a quarter century. "We are trying to catch up to you, and not the other way around," says Tokyo University Professor Tohru Moto-oka, who organized the project for the Japanese government. Although the Japanese are highly regarded as superb engineers, Japanese computer scientists have often been faulted for failing to develop innovative computer software.

In a break with tradition, Kazuhiro Fuchi, the Fifth Generation project director, has deliberately assembled a young team: "The question was who would adapt most easily to this research," says Fuchi. "Young people have fewer fixed ideas." The project, headquartered in a downtown Tokyo skyscraper, will focus on computer architectures, software, and the symbolic logic necessary to build thinking computers. In the US, meanwhile, three huge new programs in electronics and computing are getting under way.

The Microelectronics and Computer Technology Corp. (MCC)

Last year William Norris, the founder and chairman of Control Data Corp., convened a meeting of top computer and semiconductor industry executives at the Grenelefe Golf and Tennis resort in Orlando, Florida, to discuss setting up a hugh research cooperative.

The companies agreed to form a nonprofit joint venture so that they could pool their resources and share the cost of doing long-range research. Twelve major us corporations joined the new organization, including Honeywell, Motorola, RCA, and Control Data. MCC is a bold departure from the way research is usually done in American universities and corporations, and it will probe the limits of the nation's antitrust laws. The venture partly follows the Japanese model: the companies will donate scientists and researchers to MCC, loaning them for up to four years.

The corporate co-owners will also put up the money to fund MCC' research, in return for the rights to use the results. Whether the scheme will work is an open question. The 12 companies in MCC are competitors in fast-moving, high-technology markets, and ordinarily they jealously guard any technological edge they gain. In fact, many top us firms—Cray Research, Texas Instruments, Intel, and others-chose to stay out of MCC. "That's not our style," says John A. Rollwagen, chairman of Cray Research, an 11-year old company proud of its entrepreneurial creed. "We don't want to participate." The biggest market force of all-IBM-reportedly stayed out of MCC because it feared antitrust action against it if it joined. So far, however, the creation of MCC has not provoked any such suits.

In January San Francisco antitrust lawyer Joseph M. Alioto did write to the chief executives of the companies that were about to form MCC: "In my opinion, your contemplated conduct is an unequivocal combination in violation of the antitrust laws of the United States.~' But the threat did not deter MCC's co-owners and, for the time being at least, the Justice Department has allowed the MCC plan to stand. To run the new corporation, MCC's directors chose retired Admiral Bobby Ray Inman, former director of the National Security Agency and former deputy director of the CIA. Inman is widely respected for his managerial abilities and is an adept politician besides. "The day they picked Bob Inman to head MCC," says George W. Keywork II, Ronald Reagan's top science adviser, "any concern about its success diminished in my mind."

Over the past five months, Inman orchestrated a competition among 57 cities for the MCC headquarters;

the winner was Austin, Texas, after private donors, the state, and universities put together a generous package of incentives.

The consortium will have a budget of about $75 million a year and a staff of 250. Its first projects include programs in semiconductor packaging and interconnect technology, advanced software engineering and computer-aided design and manufacturing (CAD/CAM) for the electronics and computer industries. Most ambitious is a 10-year program aimed at breakthroughs in computer architecture, software, and artificial intelligence.

MCC will own the licenses and patents to the technologies; the manufacturing and marketing will be left to the companies that sponsor the projects. MCC win give them a competitive edge on the market-they will have exclusive rights for three years before the research is published and other firms are allowed to buy licenses.

The Semiconductor Research Corp.

Over the past three years Japan has captured a vital segment of the world semiconductor industry, the market for so-called RAM (random access memory) chips, a technology invented in America.

Japan now supplies 70 percent of all 64K RAMS sold, and it appears that, as the next generation of memory chips, the 256K RAMS, is being readied for market, the Japanese semiconductor companies are threatening to take a big share of sales. It makes for a grim reminder: a decade ago, before an all-out government project to build up the industry, Japanese semiconductor firms lagged far behind American and European chip companies. Last year 13 us chip manufacturers and computer companies banded together to form a nonprofit research consortium, the Semiconductor Research Corp. (SRC), to share the spiraling costs of advanced research and development.

SRC's founders include Control Data Corp., Digital Equipment Corp., Hewlett-Packard, mm, Intel and Motorola. Unlike mcc, however, SRC, which is headquartered at Research Triangle Park in North Carolina, does not carry out its own research. Instead, it sponsors research at universities. SRC is spending $12 million this year and has allocated $30 million next year. The goal: "To assure long-term survival in the market," says Larry Sumney, SRC's executive director.

DARPA

The Pentagon's Defense Advanced Research Projects Agency (DARPA) is, more than any other single agency in the world, responsible for the shape of advanced computer science today-and for many technologies now in widespread commercial use.

Over the past 20 years, DARPA has poured half a billion dollars into computer research, in the process virtually creating the science of artificial intelligence.

The first supercomputer, built in 1964, was a DARPA project. Computer time sharing, a fundamental advance, came out of work sponsored by DARPA-, So did packet-switched networks, the workhorses of today's telecommunications data networks. And computer graphics-now used on desktop computers and video-arcade cockpits—is a DARPA-sponsored invention. DARPA's next priority is a push for advanced supercomputing and artificial intelligence technologies that may cost as much as $1 billion.

DARPA plans to do everything the Japanese have set out to accomplish-and more. Earlier this year DARPA proposed a "Strategic Computing and Survivability" project, which it hopes will lead to a variety of new machines. "We want some architectures that are good for building semantic memories, memories that can hold knowledge," says DARPA's computer director, Robert Kahn. "Other kinds of systems are good for logic processing. We want architectures that can do very rapid signal processing [and] structures that can handle very, very large amounts of data in communications."

Once they are in place, these technologies will make possible an astonishing new breed of weapons and military hardware. Smart robot weapons—drone aircraft, unmanned submarines, and land vehicles—that combine artificial intelligence and high-powered computing can be sent off to do jobs that now involve human risk. "This is a very sexy area to the military, because you can imagine all kinds of neat, interesting things you could send off on their own little missions around the world or even in local combat," says Kahn.

The Pentagon will also use the technologies to create artificial intelligence machines that can be used as battlefield advisers and superintelligent computers to coordinate complex weapons systems.

An intelligent missile guidance system would have to bring together different technologies-real-time signal processing, numerical calculations, and symbolic processing, all at unimaginably high speeds-in order to make decisions and give advice to human commanders. While the national security needs are driving supercomputing technologies, there is a growing market for commercial spinoffs.

The same technology that can be used to simulate an antitank missile smashing into a heavily armored tank can also be put to work on less martial arts. In Los Angeles, Digital Productions, Inc., is using a Cray supercomputer to produce television commercials for Mattel, rock video segments for Turner Broadcasting, and special effects for Lorimar's "Star Fighter" space epic, which will be released next summer. Instead of shooting a commercial the conventional way-a costly photo session-Digital can create the "pictures" it needs in detail so precise that it's impossible to distinguish between the supercomputer's graphic image and the real photo. For inanimate objects, that is: the Cray-1/S can simulate a car right down to the glint of sunlight on the windshield, but not a human being. As the commercial market grows, the Japanese believe that their strategy of building supercomputers for the general-purpose market will pay off.

During the past year Fujitsu, Hitachi, and NEC have each announced supercomputers faster than the most powerful American machines now on the market, the Cray X-MP and Control Data's Cyber 205. Moreover, all three are designed to use the standard Fortran language, lifted from ordinary mainframe computers, but at much faster speeds. "Although supercomputers right now are mainly being used by specialists," says Takamitsu Tsuchimoto, Fujitsu Corp.'s development manager for supercomputers, "we believe that in the next 5 to 10 years they will be used by a lot of ordinary people, so we wanted to design a machine [they could use] without making great efforts." Designing a supercomputer is no easy task. America's premier supercomputer designer is Seymour Cray, 57, who designed the Cray-I and the basic architecture of Control Data's Cyber 205.

The Cray x-mp contains a dense pack of 240,000 silicon chips arranged to shorten the distances the electrical signals must travel, thereby decreasing the time it takes to perform an operation; the new Cray x-mPs will run at 400 million operations per second. And Japan's superspeed goal is 10 billion operations per second. (An Apple IIe computer contains 31 chips and can execute 500,000 operations per second.) Because of the cost of supercomputers—Cray's x-mp will sell for $11 million-the market will remain limited. Japan's Fifth Generation project, however, plans to build "super personal computers."

These huge increases in raw computer power are just the first step. The most profound changes brought by the new technologies will be the development of reasoning computers that will use superspeed symbol manipulation to simulate human thought. "We are about to see the next explosion, which is the application of computers to reasoning," says Stanford University computer scientist Edward A. Feigenbaum, who is a founder of two artificial intelligence companies, Teknowledge Inc. and IntelliGenetics, and coauthor of a new book on Japan's challenge, The Fifth Generation.

Limited forms of artificial intelligence are already enjoying commercial success. Digital Equipment Corp. the nation's second largest computer firm, uses an AI program called X-CON to make custom designs of its, computer systems.

Using a set of more than 2500 rules programmed into the system, X-CON examines a customer's specifications, determines whether all the necessary components are included, then draws a set of diagrams showing the proper spatial relationships among the components. Scientists studying artificial intelligence have been aided by advances in computer hardware, too. In 1980 a group left MIT's Artificial Intelligence Laboratory to found a company, Symbolics Inc., of Cambridge, Mass., to build computers specially designed to run LISP, a language used to develop artificial intelligence programs; and Xerox has begun to sell similar computers. Symbolics has been selling its machines, the Symbolics 3600, to a broad range of university and industrial research labs.

The company has another customer as well: the managers running Japan's Fifth Generation project have bought 10 Symbolics machines-and they have 15 more on order. In exploring the brave new world of artificial intelligence, computer scientists are concentrating on several important problems. "Knowledge engineers" are building so-called expert systems that can mimic human expertise in a narrowly defined area. The firm of Teknowledge, in Palo Alto, California, for example, has built an expert system for the French Elf Acquitaine Oil Co., a system that will give advice on one of the industry's most costly technical problems-what to do when a drill bit gets stuck thousands of feet below the earth's surface.

To build the system, Teknowledge engineers interviewed Elf Acquitaine's top troubleshooter, Jacques-Marie Courté, and then programmed his answers into a computer. The program is, in effect, a computer replica of Courtés expertise; the computer will ask the drilling-rig foremen questions, just as Courté would.

Once it gathers the information it needs, the computer will make recommendations by drawing images on the screen and giving suggestions on how to retrieve the bit. Because daily drilling costs are high, Elf Acquitaine may well recover the program's development costs the first time it is used successfully. General Electric is building a software program that will provide expert advice on repairing locomotives.

The Pentagon would like to build artificial intelligence programs that could serve as a pilot's assistant in the cockpit. Stockbrokers and insurance agents may also soon get help: "Some people are beginning to see a gold mine in [building artificial intelligence programs for] financial services," says Patrick Henry Winston, chairman Of MIT's Artificial Intelligence Laboratory. And savvy software designers for the personal computer industry are beginning to look at artificial intelligence as the next big wave that will sweep the market. Despite the successes, there are problems ahead as researchers attempt to move beyond the building of narrowly defined "experts." "There's a lot of hard stuff out there we just don't have the answers to," says Roger Schank, director of Yale University's Artificial Intelligence Laboratory. Computers have always been maddeningly literal machines, subject to the absolute tyranny of the binary codes they use to do their calculations. (The switches are either on or off, simulating ones or zeros, nothing else.)

That literal-mindedness can transform a problem that would seem trivial to humans into a nightmare. Consider the simple statement "Mary had a little lamb."

For a computer to translate the text into another language-a function scientists are now trying to develop-it would have to sort through what is, by one count, 28 possible interpretations (Mary owned the lamb, Mary ate the lamb, Mary had sexual relations with the lamb, Mary gave birth to the lamb, and on and on).

The kind of understanding humans experience as a "flash of recognition" is also difficult to instill in a computer. The statement "Ronald Reagan is president" carries a number of immediate meanings to a flesh-and-blood American, but a computer would have to rummage through its silicon memory chips in search of dozens of facts-what the word "president" means and biographical facts and details that tell who Ronald Reagan is. And the biggest challenge of all-teaching computers to learn to acquire knowledge on their own-is nowhere near being solved.

Mankind has long been enchanted-and frightened-by the prospect of creating machines that think. "I don't see any limitations to artificial intelligence," says Nobel laureate Herbert Simon, professor of computer science and psychology at Carnegie-Mellon. "All the mechanisms for human intelligence are present. Already machines can think just like people-in a limited sense. Man isn't unique in that respect." Moreover, many machines may soon possess sight, touch, hearing (in the form of voice recognition), and speech, thus imitating humans' sensory capacities along with their intellectual ones. But whole areas of the human thought process-volition, emotion, the creative uses of error-still lie well outside a computer's experience. And scientists doing research on artificial intelligence are far from their ultimate goal-a computer-based analog of the human brain.

Still, the race to build superintelligent computers-Japan's challenge to the us-will almost certainly push the technology to new levels. "While at the beginning I was angry at Japan because I felt that they were swiping our best ideas, really, on second thoughts, I couldn't blame them," says Dertouzos of MIT. "And I don't blame them today at all. I think they're doing exactly what they should." And the Japanese challenge has at last spurred the us into action. "If we really wake up, I'm very optimistic," says Dertouzos. "We could beat the daylights out of them." No one knows where the competition will ultimately lead.

11

Software

Software—the set of instructions—that tell a computer what to do-is becoming more important than the computer itself. The booming software industry is therefore setting the pace of the information technology, revolution-and the pace is frantic. This article first appeared in Business Week, February 27, 1984. Hardware is no longer where the action is. Computers are becoming remarkably similar-in many cases they are turning into off-the-shelf commodity products. Now the computer wars are being fought on a new battleground: software-the instructions that tell computers how to do everything from processing payrolls to playing video games.

A key reason for the change in emphasis is an overwhelming demand from customers for packaged software that will let them apply computer power to a broad range of new tasks. Increasingly, corporations are-finding they do not have the resources to write the programs they need. As a result, most companies have stopped writing their own software and are instead buying standard software packages. So far, producers have been unable to keep up with the need, and there has been a severe shortage of software able to take advantage of the power of the latest machines. "We're getting the hardware [we need from the industry], but software has not moved out at the same rate," says Robert J. Metzler, vice-president of First Computer Services, the data processing arm of First Union National Bank in Charlotte, NC. "There's a tremendous cry in the industry [for software]." The flood of personal computers pouring into small businesses and homes has created an even faster-growing new market.

The booming demand for new and better programs has quickly turned software into big business. As recently as three years ago, software was stiff a cottage industry, 'with sales totaling just $2.7 billion annually. This year-according to estimates by Input, a California market research firm-sales are expected to top $10 billion.

With the industry growing that fast, several once-small software companies have become sizable corporations. Management Science America Inc. (MSA), for example, the largest independent software supplier, quadrupled in size during the past three years, topping $145 million in sales in 1983. Trying to capture some of the soaring market, thousands of new companies have entered the software business in recent years; by one count there are more than 3000 software companies now.

While over the long term a shakeout is probably inevitable, the near-term outlook for most of these companies appears extremely bright. "The upside potential has barely been tapped," says Robert M. Freeman, senior analyst at Input. He expects the market to keep growing by a dizzying 32 percent a year, topping $30 billion in 1988. Software sales of that magnitude would amount to half of the $60 billion hardware business expected for the same year; today, revenue from software is equal to only 27 percent of the value of all the computer hardware sold.

Sales of software for personal computers-the fastest-growing part of the software industry-should rise by an astounding 44 percent annually over the same five years. "We're finally at the point where software applications are going to be a big moneymaker," says Jack M. Scanlon, vice-president of the Computer Systems Div. of AT&T Technologies Inc. But with the promise of such rapid market growth has come a feverish competition that is beginning to restructure the entire industry.

Until recently, nearly all software companies concentrated on a particular niche and fit neatly into one of three distinct market segments that were divided along the same lines for both mainframe and personal computers.

Systems software, which handles basic housekeeping operations such as controlling the printer and memory, was supplied primarily by the computer makers. They were joined by independent software companies in providing utility software, which, among other things, helps programmers write programs. And a host of other independent software companies competed in the third market; applications packages, which tell a computer how to carry out specific tasks such as accounting payroll or word processing.

But those distinctions are blurring:

Consolidation

International Business Machines Corp., to move faster into applications software, in November placed all its software efforts into a single, entrepreneurial unit-the same type of organization it used to launch the highly successful Personal Computer.

Acquisitions

To provide a full complement of software for their computers, makers such as Hewlett-Packard, Burroughs, and Prime Computer are rushing to buy applications software companies. Other manufacturers, including Honey-well, Sperry, and Digital Equipment, are setting up joint ventures with software suppliers. Says Roger T. Hobbs, vice-president for software products and services at Burroughs Corp.: "The demands for software are increasing so rapidly that it is impossible for the manufacturer to keep up."

Expanding product lines

Software companies are expanding product lines to maintain their competitive edge. Those that supply programs mostly for large mainframes-MSA, Cullinet Software, and Computer Associates International, for example-are snapping up personal computer software houses. And companies that specialize in systems software for personal computers-among them, Ashton-Tate, Digital Research, and Microsoft-are adding general-purpose applications software to their product lines. "Today you have to have a broad line," says Terry L. Opdendyk, president of VisiCorp. Otherwise, "the vendor is increasingly vulnerable to competition."

New players

To grab a piece of the action, publishers and other communications companies outside the computer business-including CBS, Dow Jones, Dun & Bradstreet, McGraw-Hill, and Simon and Schuster-are licensing programs they then sell through their own distribution channels. "It's a very fragmented industry, but the potential is absolutely huge," says Richard W. Young, president of Houghton Mifflin Co.

Japan's drive

To catch up with their us rivals, Japanese computer makers are launching major software development efforts. Perhaps the best evidence of just how important software has become is the drive by Japan's Ministry of International Trade & Industry to change the law to boost Japan's fledgling software industry. One result of many of these trends is that mergers and acquisitions in the industry are at an all-time high. Last year there were 146 acquisitions, valued at more than $1 billion-up 130 percent from 1982-reports Broadview Associates, a New Jersey company handling such transactions. And this frantic pace of activity is turning the software business into a hot investment area.

To complete successfully amid all the turmoil, software suppliers are struggling to formulate new strategies. One common focus is advanced design-especially the development of software aimed at making computers easier to use. But just as important to the success of new software as advanced design is marketing. Nowhere is the new attention to marketing more noticeable than in the hotly competitive personal computer business. To reach the millions of personal computer users, software companies are spending huge amounts to introduce and advertise their products. Industry watchers have dubbed this obsession with splashy promotion "the Lotus syndrome-a reference to the more than $1 million that Lotus Development Corp. spent over a three-month period in 1983 to launch its first product, the highly successful 1-2-3 package. "Lotus advertised so much that companies are going to be forced to step up their advertising just to be heard above the noise," says David E. Gold, a San Jose (Calif.) computer consultant.

Advertising, in fact, has grown so important to software success that it has become one of the biggest barriers keeping out new companies. "The cost of technology development is dwarfed by the marketing cost; the ante has really been upped," says Rodney N. Turner, vice-president for sales at Ashton-Tate, a Culver City (Calif.) software company best known for its dBase II package. It takes as much as $8 million to launch a new software product today, he estimates. Ashton-Tate, by contrast, was founded on shoestring-$7,500. Any personal computer program must be carefully packaged and promoted. "It has to look good and has to be well supported by national advertising," maintains retailer Gregg E. Olson, a salesman at Mr Software in Boulder, Colo. "A company that wants to sell to us has to have all their marketing elements in place to establish credibility with us and our customers."

Even companies that write software for the large minicomputers and mainframes are plowing more money into marketing. While programs for the larger systems, unlike those for personal computers, do not require heavy consumer advertising, says Martin A. Goetz, senior vice-president at Applied Data Research Inc., his company still boosted its 1984 advertising budget by 60 percent over last year, to about $2 million.

This emphasis on marketing comes chiefly from the need to reach a different, far broader group of potential customers. "Ten years ago, [our customer] was the data processing department, and if you had a product, you sold it to the technicians," says Robert D. Baskerville, group vice-president for product management at Computer Sciences Corp. in El Segundo, Calif. Today, he notes, a software company has "to sell to end users, and you have to emphasize more than the technical capability-you have to really sell the benefit."

Software marketing now means beginning with detailed product planning, so that a program will better meet the needs of customers. Before Wyly Corp. even began a $20 million program to diversify into applications software, for example, it brought in all its salesmen from the field to tell programmers what customers wanted-something most software companies had never done.

"With modern software development techniques, you can produce almost perfect code, but if you don't understand the market, it could still be useless," says Ron W. Brittian, Wyly's vice-president for research and development.

Critical, too, is a reputation for good service and customer support. "To grow from a startup into a large software company is not so easy anymore; it's a question of distribution and of educating the customer in how to use the product," says Anthony W. Wang, executive vice-president at Computer Associates International Inc. Toward this end, his company recently installed a $250,000 television studio—costing $200,000 or more a year to run-to make training videotapes for its software customers.

As competition heightens and customers become more demanding, companies selling personal computer software are providing a level of customer support far greater than anything they offered even a year ago. MicroPro International Corp., for example, has plowed $2.5 million into developing computer-aided instruction and retail-support aids for its software, which includes the best-selling WordStar. The company is also hiring journalists and other nontechnical writers to produce more readable instructions for today's less sophisticated customers. "A product is not a product until you have computer-aided instruction, it's not a product until you have, video instruction, it's not a product until you have honest-to-God understandable language [in the manual]," says H. Glen Haney, president of MicroPro.

Establishing a marketing presence is especially critical to companies that provide personal computer software, because they must win space on already crowded retail shelves. Computer retailers are reluctant to take on new software without feeling confident it is a winner. "Unless we're absolutely convinced that it's a great program, we'll wait to see how other channels of distribution do with it," says John H. Rollins, national manager for Sears Business Systems Centers, the computer retailing arm of Sears, Roebuck & Co. One group trying hard to enter the software business may have an edge: the traditional book publishers. Because they already sell books to computer stores, the publishers "provide ready-made distribution channels," says Input's Freeman. Agrees William M. Graves, president of MSA: "There is a tremendous similarity in the microcomputer business and publishing."

No matter how they distribute their products, software companies are finding that they must offer a broader range of products than ever before. "The strategy is to offer a complete solution," asserts Robert N. Goldman, president of Cullinet. "If a customer ends up with eight different vendors, none of the software works together." Cullinet, for instance, is augmenting its data base management software with such applications as general ledger accounting and manufacturing control programs .

Broadening a software line also helps a supplier leverage the large amounts of money spent on establishing a reputation and brand recognition. VisiCorp, which gained market fame with its hit program VisiCalc, is trying to expand its applications software with its family of Visi On integrated software. Similarly, Microsoft is plunging into such applications software as word processing and financial analysis to build on its reputation as a supplier of personal computer operating systems.

The trend toward comprehensive offerings will force small companies to target well-defined market niches. There will continue to be demand for specialized packages designed for the needs of a particular industry or profession. "There will be several very large software companies," contends John P. Imlay Jr., chairman Of MSA, "but there will be literally hundreds of small companies, with under $100 million [in sales], that have specialized market niches."

Perhaps the most fundamental change in the software industry is the blurring distinctions among the suppliers. No longer can they be neatly divided into companies that make basic systems software and those that write programs for specific applications.

Moreover, the top mainframe software companies are rushing to market with software for personal computers. And vendors serving only the personal computer market are joining with suppliers of mainframe software. VisiCorp, for example, recently teamed up with Informatics General Corp. to offer Visi-Answer, a program that allows a user of an IBM Personal Computer to retrieve information from an IBM mainframe data base. These changes resulted in large part from the growing number of customers linking personal computers to large mainframe systems.

As the emphasis in the data processing industry shifts to software-and, as software companies strengthen their sales, service, and distribution-the big-system makers, too, are scrambling to do more to provide their customers with software. "In the old days, our customer wrote his own application [software]," notes Jon Tempas, vice-president for software products at Sperry Corp.'s Computer Systems operation.

Today, "there's an increased expectation for hardware suppliers to provide the complete solution." That means the equipment makers will need to provide more of their own software. Sperry, for example, now writes 95 percent of the software it sells for its computer line.

Most of the big-system companies, however, are turning to software specialists for help, since much of the demand is for applications software finely tuned to specific industries. "I don't think there's any hardware manufacturer that can-or should-provide all the software," says John E. Steuri, general manager of Information Services Business Unit, IBM's new independent software group. "We'll be more and more dependent over time on software developed outside the company." The pressure to team up with independent software companies is especially strong among makers of personal computers.

"Without an adequate software base, a microcomputer dies," says Eugene W. Helms, vice-president for business development at Texas Instruments Inc.'s Data Systems Group. So TI is recruiting software suppliers to adapt their best-selling programs for its Professional Computer. Perhaps the most extensive effort to sign up independent software companies was made recently by Apple Computer Inc., which courted more than 100 companies to write software for its new Macintosh computer. The California company was successful in signing up more than 80 of them.

Companies that do not move quickly to develop a broad line of software will have trouble keeping up. Consider Tymshare Inc., a computer timesharing company. As computer prices began to drop precipitously, more and more of Tymshare's customers stopped renting computer time and purchased their own machines. Tymshare did not have any software packages to sell to its former clients. "We used to look at software as simply an in-house tool that we needed to offer time-sharing," says one Tymshare executive. That attitude, he admits, "came back and bit us in the rear end." In 1983 the California company lost $1.7 million while sales fell 3 per cent to $288 million. Now it is engaged in a major effort to expand into applications software, through internal development and by licensing packages developed by other companies.

With most software companies trying hard to move

in the same direction, everyone will face stiffer competition. Already, prices for personal computer software are sliding wherever similar programs have proliferated-in electronic spreadsheets and word processors, for example. And a big battle is under way among suppliers of the various "windowing" software packages-software "environments" that permit the users of personal computers to display several tasks at once. VisiCorp has been forced to slash the price of its Visi On environment package from $495 to $95. "The consumer is going to force the prices down simply by demand," asserts Alvin B. Reuben, executive vice-president at Simon & Schuster Inc.'s electronic publishing division.

As Prices fall, the opportunity for,, newcomer to jump in and grab quick and easy profits will all but disappear. The cost of developing and marketing new programs is mushrooming just when margins are shrinking. VisiCorp successfully launched VisiCalc in 1978 with a $500 budget. But the California company has spent more than $10 million developing its latest product, the Visi On environment. Product life is also getting shorter as new products come out faster. As a result, says Softsel's Wagman, "the stakes have gotten higher and much riskier from a development point of view."

For many companies, the risks will ultimately prove fatal. "There are companies out there that are already feeling the pinch of increased costs, new product announcements, and a changing marketplace," warns consultant Gold. Industry watchers predict that some big-name failures will occur within the next 18 months. By the end of the decade, many experts expect the software industry to have consolidated its thousands of suppliers into a few major players.

For those that make it, the future is promising. The demand by the growing army of computer users for easier-to-use software to handle an exploding variety of tasks will drive the industry to create software with far more capabilities than anything available today. "They only limit," says Stuart A. Walker, vice-president of marketing at Konware Inc., "is the limit of new ideas."

Software in the Office

One of the main reasons software has become so highly visible is that the computer has moved from the back room into the office.

Programs of the Past, buried inside corporate data Processing centers, primarily handled clerical and accounting tasks, such as turning out payrolls and keeping track of accounts receivable. Today's Computer handles a rapidly increasing variety of management tasks—employing information as a competitive marketing weapon, for example.

That trend, coupled with the explosion in the use Of Personal computers by executives, has given new prominence and importance to software in us corporations. "The Programs that we install to do Our company's business are analogous to the tools an auto maker Puts in place to manufacture auto parts," says Jeffry A. Alperin, an assistant vice-president in the Information Systems Support Dept at Aetna Life & Casualty Co. "Our plant is our data Processing system." Since the same computer hardware is available to everyone it is the software that often gives a company a competitive edge. At oil companies, software is now helping drive the search for oil and gas," says Michael C. Balay, general manager of information technology at Gulf Oil Corp. "You can have the same [seismic] information, but a unique software package may help you better interpret the data. "

Nowhere is this increasing importance More obvious than in corporate data processing budgets. Belay estimates that Gulf spends about half of its annual data processing budget to write its own software and to buy packages from independent suppliers. At Aetna, half of the 4000 people on the data processing staff are programmers. And Alperin says that 4 percent of the $237 million that Aetna spent on information processing last year went to purchase packaged software.

Moreover, individual owners of personal computers are no different from large corporations: over the life of a computer, its owner will spend $2 on software for every $1 spent on hardware, according to industry estimates. But users are finding it increasingly difficult to produce their own programs. Writing software is still a time-consuming process, and users find that, while they want to employ their computers to handle more applications they do not have enough programmers, time, or money to write all of the necessary software in-house. In fact at many companies users must now wait as long as 18 months for new programs to be written. "The end users are demanding faster development of solutions," declares Richard R. Douglas, group vice-president for the us Marketing and Services Group of Honeywell Inc.

To come up with this software faster, computer users are compromising-buying more ready-to-run software packages than ever before. "There has been a turnaround from five or six years ago," says James T. Manion, sales vice-president at ASK Computer Systems Inc. Few computer users write all their own programs anymore, he says. But while users sacrifice some uniqueness by buying a software package, that disadvantage is often outweighed by the time and money saved. A package can cut the time it takes to get a system up and running by more than half, figures Mayford L. Roark, executive director of systems at Ford Motor Co. He also estimates that buying a program from an outside vendor can cut development costs by 30 to 75 percent. "It's almost impossible to think of a function you might want to do on a computer that you can't find several software packages for," says Roark.

Where a custom solution to a problem is required, companies often find they can save time by modifying a standard software package for their own use. That is what Aetna did when it needed software to offer a new type of life insurance called universal life, which features flexible premiums. That allowed the company to match its competitors' universal life offerings quickly. With such a variety of software available, companies are finding that writing their own programs from scratch makes about as much sense as drawing their own road maps for their salesmen.

Us corporations brought percent more software packages last year than in the previous year, says International Data Corp., a market researcher. Such purchases, along with software services, now account for more than 8 percent of the average data processing budget, up from 6 percent in 1980, IDC says. Similarly, purchases of personal computer software packages soared 74 per cent last year to top $1 billion, according to market researchers at California's Input.

The customer's new attitude toward software is beginning to alter fundamentally the way that computer systems are sold. "We're selling to a much more sophisticated consumer base than in the past," points out Elizabeth M. R. Hall, product manager at Information Science Inc., a Montvale (NJ) software company. From now on, adds Honeywell's Douglas, "Software looms as a much more important factor in [a user's purchase] decision than hardware."

Computing used to be the solitary domain of a priesthood of programmers. The arcane languages that they employed to command their giant mainframe systems were shrouded in such 'complexity that few laymen could understand, much less control, these behemoths. But the inexpensive yet powerful personal computer is changing all that. Millions of nontechnical users are now running computers. These new operators, however, refuse even to read an instruction manual, let alone memorize the cryptic commands of the priesthood. Their aversion, coupled with the dramatic slide in the cost of computer power, has created a revolution in the way software is written.

Today, making a program simple to control and easy to use is just as important as what the program actually does. Says Jeanne M. Baccash, a software engineer at American Telephone & Telegraph Co.'s Bell Laboratories: "There's a whole new thrust to reach a market that doesn't know or care what it means to 'boot a system' [start a computer].

These efforts to make software simpler are crucial if the information processing industry is to continue its fast growth. "Rapidly advancing technology has left consumers, trainers, and computer salesmen behind," says Terry L. Opdendyk, president of VisiCorp. "How to spread the word of how to use the products is the key limiting factor [to the industry's growth]."

Man-machine communications

To reduce the number of commands that a user must memorize and type into a computer to get it to work, the latest software enables users to communicate with the machine in new ways. Some of these techniques are relatively simple, such as establishing menus to show users what commands are available to choose from. The most elaborate methods, used on such machines as Apple Computer Inc.'s new Macintosh, replace commands with an array of tiny icons or pictures-for example, a file folder to indicate filing. To tell the computer what to do, users point to the appropriate picture on the screen by moving a pointing device called a "mouse" over a desktop.

Data exchange

Early programs were built to accomplish tasks, such as calculating financial forecasts, with only the data located within the user's own computer. But users have grown more sophisticated and now want to get data stored in other machines-say, the corporation's central mainframe system.

Artificial intelligence

This embryonic method of programming, which enables software to mimic human thought more closely, might one day be the easiest approach to use. It is starting to show up in programs such as Artificial Intelligence Corp.'s Intellect and Microrim Corp.'s CLIO, which let a user ask a computer for data with English sentences rather than esoteric commands.

Most programmers are ill-equipped to figure out how office workers and other nontechnical users best handle computers. So companies are bringing in professionals from disciplines as far afield as education and psychology to help in the design of man-to-machine communications. AT&T, for example, had a staff of psychologists survey about 400 computers users to help it decide how to add commands to its Unix operating system. Designing easier-to-use software also requires new development techniques. For instance, International Business Machines Corp. now tests its new software in "usability labs." In these labs, volunteers try to use IBM software while researchers with video cameras watch from behind one-way mirrors. "In the long haul, those that have easy-to-understand software will be the successful companies," says John E. Steuri, general manager of IBM's Information Services Business Unit.

A lot of discussion is going on in research circles over how best to use menus, pictograms, and other techniques to help both computer novices and experts. The type of coaching that a neophyte computer user requires becomes annoying once the user has learned to use the software. So designers want "to make sure the user is not presented with extraneous information when he has to decide what to do next," says Brian K. Reid, a Stanford University electrical engineering professor. Micropro International Corp., for one, is trying to solve this problem by using a time-delay activator.

If a user types in a command less than two seconds after being asked for it, the program assumes the user is proficient and skips over the menu listing of options. Users who take longer are given the benefit of directions from a menu. Researchers are also struggling with the problem of how to standardize commands. Each computer program now uses different commands to accomplish the same function. An early attempt to solve this problem is the "environment" or "windowing" software packages for personal computers that are now coming to market. These packages-products such as Microsoft Corp's Windows and VisiCorp's Visi On-divide the computer screen into segments, each of which shows a different task. Common functions are performed the same way in each window. The large amount of this kind of innovative software now being developed to make personal computers easier to use is also forcing the mainframe software companies to follow suit. "Mainframe vendors have been forced to make software easier' because users have been spoiled by micros," says David Ferris, an industry consultant.

Information Builders Inc. has developed a version of its Focus data base management software that can run on an IBM Personal Computer. But the PC version, called Pc-Focus, "has more features than the mainframe product because after using a personal computer customers have come to expect more," says Gerald D. Cohen, president of the New York company. One of the Pc-Focus features is called Table Talk. Each time a user moves from one step to another in the course of retrieving information from a data base, the computer automatically presents him with a menu of the appropriate choices.

Another software challenge is to find simpler ways to exchange data between programs. In most cases, swapping data between a large mainframe and a personal computer is difficult because the two units use different formats for storing their data and different commands for retrieving them.

The problem is similar to that of a person who is trying to communicate with 10 people, each of whom speaks a different language, explains Robert J. Spinrad, director of systems technology at Xerox Corp. "I could either learn all nine other languages," he says, "or we could all learn a common one-say, Latin." But software vendors are not waiting until everyone in the industry agrees on what common language all computers should learn. In the past year a host of vendors, including Cullinet Software, Informatics General, and Cincom Systems, have announced products that link personal computers to large mainframes. Such capabilities will be a requisite for any software in the marketplace, says President Frank H. Dodge of McCormack & Dodge Corp. "If mainframe software doesn't allow that link," he adds, "it's going to be pushed aside pretty rapidly."

Some experts think the ultimate mechanism for exchanging data is the use of sophisticated file-management software, often called data base management systems. These large programs index information and then store it in such a way that it can be retrieved using a variety of names-much the way a library card catalog lists the same book by author, subject, and title. By providing this uniform filing structure, a data base system simplifies the exchange of data.

What may soon make computers even easier to use

is artificial intelligence (AI) software. Some companies are already working on AI programs that will eventually be able to remember an individual's habits in using the computer. The first AI applications from Microsoft-expected within the next year-will be likely to use these rudimentary pattern-recognition techniques in tutorial programs that teach novices how to operate software. These programs will adjust the level of tutorial difficulty by determining the proficiency of the student running the program. Says Microsoft Chairman William H. Gates: "Just as humans take actions based on past experience without having to be told again, and again, so will software.

As the second-largest group of computer companies in the world-after the us-they exported $2.7 billion worth of computers last year. But in their single-minded determination to build and export hardware that is faster and less expensive, the Japanese have given short shrift to software development. "Hardware manufacturers have been lazy about developing software," acknowledges Hisao Ishihara, managing director of the Japan Software Industry Assn. But now, he points out, "that is suddenly changing." Faced with the twin problems of rapidly falling hardware prices and the growing percentage of computer budgets being spent on software, Japanese hardware makers are scrambling to shift their resources into software development.

Three years ago, for example, Hitachi Ltd's Computer Division spent just 10 per cent of its research and development budget on software. This year, even though software will account for about 10 percent of its computer revenues, Hitachi will spend 30 percent of its R&D money on software. "These days, more and more of the value added in information processing comes from the software," says Toshimitsu Kaihatsu, head of Toshiba Corp.'s Software Management Dept.

The Japanese are also keenly aware that to continue to be competitive internationally in computers they must now start developing world-class software. "We have to sell more overseas if we want to recover our software development costs," comments Shoichi Ninomiya, general manager of Fujitsu Ltd.'s Information Processing Group. His company now spends close to $100 million a year-more than one-third Of its R&D budget-to develop software for its mainframe computers. But almost all of that software is now sold to Japanese customers. Until now, software has been the biggest handicap the Japanese have had in selling their equipment abroad-especially in the office and personal computer markets. This point was driven home in 1982 when International Business Machines Corp. sued Hitachi, one of the largest Japanese exporters of computers, charging the company with copying IBM software and reselling it with Hitachi's machines.

Hitachi agreed in an out-of-court settlement to pay IBM between $2 million and $4 million a month in software license fees and agreed to let the us computer giant inspect all new Hitachi products before they go on the market to ensure that they do not infringe any IBM copyrights. To avoid a similar lawsuit, Fujitsu has also agreed to pay IBM many millions of dollars and promised not to copy the us company's software, although it would not disclose the details of its agreement. Because of language and cultural differences, software written in Japan is obviously difficult to export. Not only must instruction manuals be translated, but often the programs have to be completely rewritten. Japanese accounting rules, for example, are different from those in the us, so accounting software written in Japan is useless in the us. This shortage of programs has severely limited the export potential of Japanese home and personal computers.

Japan's software industry is also held back by the preference of Japanese buyers for custom software rather than the standard software products that us customers are increasingly buying.

As a result, an independent Japanese software industry has been slow to develop. And the computer manufacturers' efforts to develop all the software themselves have been crimped by the large sums they must invest to improve methods of getting information into the computer and processing it, using Japanese *kanji* characters. But it would be dangerous to write off the Japanese as competitors in world-class software. "The Japanese are as dedicated to computers as they were to autos and shipbuilding," says John P. Imlay Jr, chairman of Management Science America Inc. "If us companies do not innovate and supply quality products and customer support, the Japanese could make inroads."

Already, Japan has a big chunk of the us market for the simplest type of software, that written for video games. Cultural differences are not a barrier to the export of such hit games as Pac-Man. The fast-growing software markets for engineering and scientific applications-which manipulate schematic drawings and numbers rather than words-are other areas where Japanese software could be sold overseas with little modification. The Japanese have also demonstrated their technical ability by creating powerful supercomputer software and sophisticated banking and airline reservation systems. "People are misreading the capability of the Japanese when they say Japanese can't build good software," maintains Joseph C. Berston, president of Comstute Inc., a software consulting firm based in Japan.

Indeed, Japanese companies may actually have some advantages over their us rivals. Because of the legendary thoroughness of Japanese workers, "the finished product here is better, more reliable, and easier to maintain," says consultant Berston. Labor costs are also lower for Japanese software makers. Well-educated, highly disciplined Japanese programmers are paid an average of about $10,000 a year. Their us counterparts can expect a starting salary twice that-from $19,000 to $25,000 according to a survey by Robert Half International Inc., a personnel agency.

In addition to that salary differential, the Japanese claim their programmers are 10 to 15 percent more productive than their us counterparts because of Japanese investments in program development aids. To widen that margin, they are now building software factories that give their programmers access to even more sophisticated tools.

Toshiba recently completed a factory that employs 3000 software engineers to develop industrial software. Now the company is building a second software factory that will employ 2000 more programmers. "To overcome Japan's language problem and compete with the us," says Toshiba's Kaihatsu, "we have to have productivity double that of the us." NEC Corp., which already spends a significant portion of its annual $400 million software budget on productivity tools, says it will use its productivity and quality advantages to crack the us market. It has hired us software engineers to analyze the needs of us computer users. The resulting lists of requirements are then fed into computers at NEC's Japanese software factories, where programmers write the software. In this fashion, NEC has already started developing commonly used business applications, says Yukio Mizuno, an NEC vice-president. Perhaps the best illustration of the importance the Japanese now attach to software is the move by the Ministry of International Trade & Industry (MITI) to back the industry. MITI has set up several research laboratories to work on software, including a lab that is developing the so-called fifth-generation computer and software. That lab is budgeted to receive $23 million in MITI support this year. The ministry is also giving low-interest loans and tax breaks to software developers.

MITI hopes to boost its fledgling software industry further with a proposed revision in the copyright law.

The ministry is pushing to allow Japanese companies to save money and programming time by making it legal for them to copy portions of existing software products without the permission of the original developers.

Industry observers say the law, if passed, would help the Japanese leapfrog us software companies by enabling them to copy popular us programs and incorporate them into Japanese software products. But even with MITI's help, it will be a long time before Japan's software industry catches up with its us competitors-if it ever does. In 1982, the latest year for which figures are available, software sales in Japan were only $1.4 billion-just one-quarter of the total us software sales that year.

12

Networking Education

Private data networks, academic and research networks have been a major influence on the development of information applications in wide area networking, since they offer a venue for experimentation and co-operative activity less constrained by strict commercial viability; the network is normally funded at a national level, by institutional subscription, or through co-operative arrangements, and thus access appears to be free at the point of use. The 1980s have seen a steady broadening both of those able to access research networks and in the range of information services and facilities available, as the network infrastructure has developed.

In some cases, it appears that the research network may form the basis of a new generation of high capacity, fast broadband networks offering widespread public access.

Research networks, by their nature, are mostly composed of a collection of co-operating autonomous institutions: organizations involved in higher education and research institutes. The management of research networks tends to reflect this structure by the way in which control is distributed amongst the participants.

Technical control lies with the network 'hubs', those institutions which provide the basic backbone of the network and the major routing facilities, or with a management group specifically set up to control the development and standardization of facilities. This kind of group may exercise control over organizations which can attach to the network, but will not control the registration of individual users, and will not at present maintain any central directory of all users.

Similarly, services which are available over the network are the responsibility of the individual institutions which offer them, as is local control over which types of user are allowed access to these. Although the degree of decentralization will vary across different networks, in relation to the primary source of funding, there is generally no single central locus of control which determines all aspects of network use. There are, therefore, no centrally maintained directories or lists of all the services which might be available; it is up to the individual user to discover this information for themselves, perhaps aided by information or resource tools created through the initiative of other users, often on a rather *ad hoc* basis.

Navigating, through a research network is, at the moment, a matter of individual learning and initiative, presenting a steep learning curve to novice users. This barrier extends not only to knowledge of the specific facilities which might be available, but also to the way in which these facilities can be used on different computers and software systems, which may vary tremendously from one site to another.

The basic information services which are offered by research networks fall into three main categories. *Information exchange* services allow individuals and groups to communicate with each other across time zones and geographical space much more quickly than postal delivery would allow, and has proved the most popular and heavily used end-user application on networks by linking together people who would otherwise find it hard to meet face to face.

— *Electronic mail* facilities enable the exchange of messages and ideas on a one-to-one basis, whether more formally as in the sharing of notes and drafts of work-in-progress, or informally for general social contact.

— *Discussion groups* which use electronic mail in conjunction with mailing lists support the exchange of information and messages between all members of a group at the same time. This is popular for ongoing debates and the exchange of news items in discipline-specific areas, allowing members to share ideas and experiences in an informal setting, to 'meet' new contacts, and to follow and influence the development of new ideas in their field.

— *Bulletin boards* are used in discipline-specific settings, but require a positive action from the user in connecting to the service, and reading or downloading items of interest, rather than depending on the blanket distribution of material through mailing lists.

— *Computer conferencing* and interactive video-conferencing are still quite rare activities on such networks, but will become increasingly common as the technical infrastructure becomes capable of real-time interactive and multimedia services, and are likely to have substantial implications for distance learning education.

File and document distribution support the distribution of items such as text documents, image files, and software programs on an individual search and retrieve basis.

File transfer is permitted by the use of standard protocols so that data files can quickly be moved from one machine to another under the control of the end-user. As more electronic material is becoming available within the public domain, certain computer network sites offer an 'archive' service, in which data files can be stored on open access for retrieval by all network users.

Mail servers are commonly used as primitive database systems, returning files in response to commands received within electronic mail messages, as an automatic process with no manual intervention. This is often the method used for distribution of the composite articles within an electronic journal, for example—the user will request a particular file by name by placing the appropriate commands and filename within a mail message addressed to the mail server.

Information services are available through remote log-in protocols, which allow the user to link to a remote system and use it as though there were a direct connection between the two, within the constraints set by the host system. The service may be on a different network, as long as both end systems (user and host) are able to run the same protocols, and the networks and gateway used will support this.

Online public access catalogues available for remote searching from outside the library or campus site are a common use for this facility, as long as the OPAC allows for a remote connection. There is, of course, no common standard interface for the various online catalogues and so the user must know, or be able to learn, the functions and abilities of each different system.

Non-bibliographic databases are increasingly becoming available across research networks, particularly those which contain information within the public domain, or government-sponsored public information. Once again there is no standard searching approach, and the format and content of the databases may be very different.

The full range of academic and research networks worldwide includes both large- and small-scale networks at differing stages in their development, and is too numerous to list here. Most research networks are organized on a national basis, or as a cooperative endeavour between smaller countries, as for example in the Gulf states. A comprehensive directory of networks is given in the books by Quarterman and LaQuey, together with a summary of protocols used, and a description of network interconnections.

The European academic and research networks are brought together in *RARE*(Reseaux Associes pour la Recherche Europeenne), the association for European research networking organizations and their users. This aims to overcome national boundaries in research networking by creating a harmonized computer communications infrastructure for the whole European research community. Based in Amsterdam, RARE has over 40 national and international research networking organizations as members, which are listed and described in the RARE 'State of the union' report. '

The RARE association also sponsors a number of working groups which initiate and co-ordinate advances in network technology and services; these include, for example, work on user support issues, information retrieval across the networks, and developing multimedia services. The academic network for the United Kingdom is called *JANET* (Joint Academic Network). Similar networks exist for nearly all the other European countries, including Eastern Europe, although the range of facilities which each is able to offer can vary widely; in some former Communist countries, such as Romania, access is very difficult and services are unreliable. Others are far more highly developed, with extensive experience and expertise, and are moving towards a strategic position of greater independence from government support and self-sufficiency.

The Dutch academic network, *SURFnet*, is an example within this category. SURFnet networks together institutes of higher education, and scientific and industrial research organizations in the Netherlands, and has maintained a close involvement with the Dutch bibliographic utilities, taking a pro-active approach to the development of information services.

In 1989 SURFnet became a private company, with a 49% share held by the Dutch telecommunications company PTT Telecom, and was required to become self-supporting in the near future. This has led it into substantial development in services and user support, working on-site with institutions and with individual discipline-based groups of users between institutions, to encourage and develop new users and uses for the network. There are several other major influences and initiatives which affect the shape of European academic networking at a transnational level, both outside and within the EC. These include:

Organizations which are co-operative efforts between countries grouped together by geography. *NORDUnet* is a collaborative effort between the Scandinavian group of national research networks: Denmark, Finland, Norway, Sweden, and Iceland aiming to enable an efficient connection to the rest of Europe. A similar arrangement has been proposed for the countries in the area of the former Yugoslavia.

EUnet is a large subscription-funded network, which serves European users from Scandinavia and the CIS (former Soviet Union) to North Africa. Founded by the European Forum for Open Systems, EUnet connects 6000 individual sites and networks together as Unix system users.

International treaty organizations which are established as European-wide enterprises, with funding from a number of countries. The most influential of these is CERN, the European Laboratory for Particle Physics, which has constructed *HEPnet* as a dedicated network serving research centres in high energy physics.

Ebone is the European backbone network, which provides a neutral interconnection between the backbone research networks which form part of the global TCP/IP based Internet described later in this chapter. The backbone provides a high capacity 'highway' between the major first-level nodes in Europe (Stockholm, Amsterdam, Geneva, Paris, and London) to which other sites connect.

EuropaNet has developed from an EC-funded project conducted by COSINE (Co-operation for Open Systems Interconnection Networking), intended to develop a co-ordinated approach to networking the European research community, and provide an international infrastructure accessible by academic organizations, research institutes, and organizations co-operating with EC research and development. A pilot International X.25 Infrastructure (IXI) network commenced in 1990, forming a backbone which linked research networks in many countries, both inside and outside the EC itself. This has now been replaced by EuropaNet as a high capacity multi-protocol backbone which will handle both OSI (open system) and TCP/IP Internet-style protocols.

The *EARN* (European Academic Research Networks) association provides networking services for researchers and academics in Europe, the Middle East and Africa, as a store and forward network based on IBM computers. EARN is closely ,integrated with the US-based BITNET network, and is in fact almost indistinguishable from this in use, effectively acting as its European arm. In some countries EARN forms the major research network, while in others there is a gateway connection between EARN and the national network.

There are three main international research networks with worldwide coverage, which are normally accessible from national-based networks, and which are based in or emanate from the United States.

The *Internet* described later in this chapter, is the largest of these; based in the US, it now has extensive worldwide coverage. The Internet is beginning to assume a quasi-public status, and is currently the subject of wide-ranging legislative attention.

BITNET is a major US-based co-operative computer network interconnecting over 3000 academic and research institutions in more than 35 countries, as far apart as Eastern Europe, Latin America and the Far East; the network encompasses a number of more local networks within its structure. BITNET was originally funded by the IBM corporation in the early 1980s, and was free to the academic community; this support is now terminated, and access is through institutional subscription. BITNET has close links with the Internet, and many sites are accessible through both networks, almost indistinguishably.

Usenet is a loose assemblage of Unix-based sites, including many thousands of computers, from large systems to personal workstations. It is strongly associated with the Unix world, and has an independent and co-operative spirit, with no central management or control, depending on allegiance to a code of good practice; the nature of Unix systems tends to limit the appeal of Usenet to a fairly specialist community.

The main feature of Usenet is the large number of discussion and newsgroups which exist within it, known as Network News, amounting to almost 30 Megabytes of 'news' daily. Essentially Usenet is not a technical data network, and does not have separate fixed lines between sites; it is more of an informal, agreement for the exchange and passing on of 'news' achieved by a variety of means, including dial-up over the public data network. Much of Usenet activity is now carried out via the Internet.

JANET, the Joint Academic Network, is an X.25 packet-switched service which provides inter-site access for and on behalf of the UK higher education and research community. Initially formed to support scientific data processing, JANET has since expanded to encompass a fundamental role as a communications medium for the academic and research communities as a whole, and now includes a broad range of information services and resources.

JANET was formed in 1984 through a rationalization of the existing academic and research networks which were established at that time in the UK. These included the two national research networks which belonged to the Science and Engineering Research Council and the Natural Environment Research Council, together with eight regional university-based networks.

Since these networks did not all work to the same standards, the introduction of an overall team for management and development of the network was required. The management and control of JANET is currently based at the SERC Rutherford Appleton laboratory in Oxfordshire: the joint network team deals with policy and development matters, and with management of the network infrastructure. Control of the local site facilities and their use of JANET, and administration of the physical connections to the JANET network, is the responsibility of the local representatives; however, these responsibilities must be fulfilled as a condition of connection to the network.

JANET provides the infrastructure which connects the facilities of its users together, rather than determining day to day use of the network. In 1993, JANET is funded by the joint information systems committee of the UK Higher, Education Funding Councils on behalf of the research and educational institutions, by top-slicing a part of the overall national budget for higher education before it is devolved to institutions.

The network is thereby provided as a general educational and research facility, essentially funded through government agency. Organizations which have been permitted to connect to JANET but which do not fall within this category pay an annual subscription fee. It is expected that in the near future, the management of JANET will be taken over by UKERNA, the UK Educational and Research Networking Association; this represents a move away from direct central government funding. Restrictions on the type of organization which can connect to JANET have been slowly relaxed over time, as the needs of JANET's primary users demand a wider range of networking contacts.

Within the 'guidelines for acceptable use' which require that network usage is related to educational and research purposes, rather than to a directly profit-making enterprise, institutions with primary connections can now allow local secondary users to connect to JANET using their primary connection as an entry node. At the present time, the guidelines allow the following kinds of organizations to directly connect to the network:

— universities and other higher education and research institutes which are funded by a central government agency;

— government research establishments not directly funded;

— not-for-profit organizations engaged in collaborative research with higher education institutes;

— libraries and related organizations, including the national libraries and the UK bibliographic utilities;

— educational councils and research institutes;

— learned societies;

— commercial organizations involved in collaborative research, or providing a service or support to higher education (for example Blackwell's periodicals service).

The JANET network developed as an X.25 (84) packet switching technology as the underlying data transmission scheme. The recent upgrading of data lines has increased the bandwidth capacity to 2 Mbps on most sites, by the use of leased lines from Mercury Communications.

At the inception of a formal JANET service in 1984, X.25 was the only realistic, choice within the European market which was able to offer wide connectivity and reasonable performance, and which was compatible with public telecommunications, while avoiding the pitfalls of proprietary protocols. Since this time, however, the alternative approach of TCP/IP has emerged as a strongly supported protocol within the research community, affecting forward planning of JANET services.

The higher level network functions were originally provided by the proprietary *Coloured Book Software* protocols, designed as an interim measure. This set of protocols provide the basic network services; the Grey Book defines an electronic mail service, for example, and the Blue Book deals with file transfer. The network administration has had the long-term goal of making a transition to the use of OSI protocols; some services, such as X.400 mail, are already available. The development of a Domain Name Server provides a name to address translation to make network connections more transparent for the end user. This is made possible by a Name Registration Scheme (NRS) which maintains a directory of the individual systems which are JANET-accessible on all the 200 or so UK sites (and some others); these have both a network address (a string of numerals prefixed by 0000) and a more usable network name.

The naming scheme can be used by local nodes to distinguish between different machines at the same site by progressively structuring the address into smaller sub-domains. Thus, a full JANET address name will identify the *uk* geographical area, followed by an *ac* to denote the academic network, a single word name for the institution as a whole, and any necessary sub-units in the organization, until an actual machine name is identified (for example, the address *uk. ac. oxbridge. cc. vaxe).* All network node names are registered on the central database, which can be downloaded into local data storage and used by name servers at individual sites.

Individual users are registered on their local machines, and any others to which they have log-in rights, by the naming convention chosen by the individual site. Information objects addressed to a specific username (for example *user@uk. ac. oxbridge. cc. vaxe)* will be delivered to the site by the network; the local system is then responsible for delivering the data to the workspace of the local user.

The basic services of electronic mail, remote log-in and file transfer have given rise to a wide range of different specialized services and access to information resources which are available to all JANET users.

The academic community which JANET serves includes a wide variety of disciplines, many of which are not traditionally linked with computer and information usage. Electronic mail, as well as serving for one to one interpersonal messaging, is often used to support group communication and as a simple interface to online information services.

The Networked Information Services Project (NISP), based at Newcastle University, was set up to explore the possibilities for enhancing, group communication and information dissemination facilities on JANET, with a particular emphasis on drawing in those groups not yet familiar with computer networking. This has led to the development, from 1989 onwards, of a mail server service known as *Mailbase*. Working with groups of academics and researchers from areas as diverse as music, history and library management, Mailbase aims to provide groups with the ability to participate in focused discussions by joining e-mail based discussion lists, each limited to a narrow topic; and for groups to run these information services themselves. Each list has an owner, responsible for managing it, and may be 'open' to public access, or 'closed' to all except invited participants; the degree of access to archived discussion can also be controlled.

Contact with the service is through the sending and receipt of electronic mail messages to the mail server based at Newcastle, and can be done from any JANET site. Some of the lists are working on specific tasks—the development of network training materials, for example—the results of which are made publicly available as retrievable documents from the Mailbase service.

As of 1992, the project reported some 6,000 users of this service, with a total of 12,000 subscriptions to the 200 existing lists. Membership of lists varies from several hundred to single figures. One of the most enthusiastic users of this service has been the academic library community, which formed a number of lists on specific topics, most of which have now merged together under the name of *lis-link.* This generates some 5-10 messages per day, providing a forum for sharing ideas and experiences, seeking answers to specific reference questions, and testing opinion on library-related issues; with the advantage of fast response from other users.

The interchange on discussion lists is normally carried out from within the familiar mail package of local systems, with no requirement for the user to be aware of delivery and connection details. Remote log in is available by invoking the calling facilities of the JANET PAD (the local link into the X.25 packet switching system), and using the local workstation as though it were a terminal with direct connection to a distant system.

In many cases, the called computer will require the caller to have a registered username and password before making any facilities accessible. Some services, however, have been set up for general access by JANET users and do not require a caller to declare an identity.

Bulletin boards require the user to connect to the systems and choose items of interest typically organized under a multi-level menu structure; documents can be read on-screen, or dispatched to the user's home system. Examples of successful bulletin boards on JANET are the Joint Network Team news service, *JANET.news; HUMBUL,* a bulletin board for users in humanities disciplines; *History.news;* and the Bulletin Board for Libraries, *BUBL.* This latter is a library-oriented information service, containing news, events, announcements, current information on networking issues, and network training materials. The bulletin board also offers a current awareness service, by listing the contents pages of relevant periodicals, and acts as a forum for the sharing of ideas and expertise on a range of LIS topics. Although still used by a relatively low proportion of the library community, BUBL achieved a usage rate of 2400 per month in January 1993.

Online public access catalogues (OPACs) of the educational member institutions are normally available to anonymous remote users through a JANET connection, which enables access to the system as though from within the library itself, though this may entail some degradation in the quality of the user interface. At least 60 UK library catalogues are available in this way, and these include those of the larger research libraries; details are listed in a directory by Peter Stone. Access to the new British Library online catalogue is likely to be available from late 1993.

A recent development is the mounting of the Institute for Scientific Information Citation Indexes for science, social sciences, and the humanities, and the Excerpta Medica database, as a JANET resource. This is accessible under the name of *BIDS* (Bath Information and Data Services). BIDS provides unlimited access to these indexes to all members of academic institutions which have paid an annual subscription fee. For the individual institution, the service is an interesting alternative to offering equivalent access through CD-ROM databases mounted on a local area network.

An added advantage of the JANET access method is that it will be able to extend the service to include document delivery as well as citation retrieval options as these become available. The British Library intends to offer a new table of contents database, Inside Information, through the BIDS service containing article descriptions from the 10,000 most requested titles from the Document Supply Centre, linked to online ordering facilities. There are a number of other databases available through the network, containing various types of non-bibliographic information: for example, the Biron database contains information on datasets held by the ESRC (Economic and Social Science Research Council), and the HENSA archive gives access to public domain software.

Several fee-charging databases and electronic resources are also available, including access to the British Library *BLAISE* service and to major online bibliographic databases. This has the advantage to the user of saving on telecommunications' costs, since use of JANET as a carrier is effectively free to the end-user. The JANET User Group for Libraries (JUGL), one of the user groups which advises the network management, has overseen the development of a library-oriented guide describing many of the resources available over JANET through *Project Jupiter*, and has contributed to network training initiatives in this area. This has helped with the navigational problems in pointing to the existence and location of useful resources, and has helped to firmly establish JANET as a medium for reference of information resources within the library environment.

The JUGL user group has also initiated the *Plan for Library Action on NETworks* (PLANET) in an attempt to encourage library and information workers to become actively involved in developing and exploiting network resources and services through an awareness of and involvement in existing projects, and the encouragement of discussion and debate on future developments.

Interactive gateways allow a user to connect to a service on a different network, and to perform searches within these services interactively, by translating from

JANET into the protocols running on the other network. This is particularly attractive for JANET users who wish to make use of Internet facilities, and are otherwise unable to do so. These gateways act as guest intermediate systems, which are connected to both networks; to search an Internet database, for example, a JANET user first contacts the appropriate gateway, and from there initiates a second link, which is controlled by the gateway computer, to the destination—the information exchange between the two end systems is conducted in two stages.

JANET gateways enable the use of remote log-in and file transfer with Internet systems in this way; the user is able to nominate the desired destination through the addressing scheme. The *NISS gateway* (National Information on Software and Services) is a more specific service offering links to specified information systems, both commercial and non-commercial, through hierarchical menus listed on sets of screens. Some of these services are freely available to all users, and others require previous registration and the use of a password and identifier.

The advantage of the gateway is that several popular services are brought together under one umbrella, without the need for special knowledge on methods of connection on the part of the user; some of the physical connections offered include services outside the UK which may not otherwise be available from all user sites. In the section on bibliographic services, the NISS gateway offers links to Datastar and Dialog bibliographic hosts; to the German DIMDI biosciences online and STN scientific and technical network; to the OCLC EPIC reference databases in Ohio, and the US Research Libraries Group Citadel system; to the ARTTel system of the British Library Document Supply Centre; to the MELVYL catalogue of the University of California, and the CARL database in Colorado; and to the Data Distribution

Network of the European Space Agency. Neither research nor educational work is limited by national boundaries, and it is desirable to extend the communicative abilities networking offers beyond these geographic limits. JANET achieves this by the use of public gateways to other major networks, falling into two principal groups.

The *public data network* (known as the PSS) gateway enables stations on JANET to link into systems that are only available in this way, without the need to reconnect to a different network at the user end. This also offers a route into JANET for those who do not belong to one of the member institutions. As a part of a public telecommunications system, use of the gateway itself is charged for by British Telecom, although activity within JANET itself is not.

Relay gateways provide links with other major research networks in Europe and the United, States. These do not offer a direct connection to services on the other network, but electronic messages and files can be passed from one network to the other, performing any necessary translation in the process, in a store and forward manner. This allows JANET users to exchange information with network users worldwide, and with relative case, although the addressing system is more complicated.

— The *Earn-Relay* gateway exchanges information packets with BITNET and EARN network services;

— The *Nsfnet-Relay* gateway performs a similar service for destinations on the Internet;

— *MHS-Relay* is an X.400 gateway giving access to Telecom Gold 400 for electronic mail messages in this format, and to an IBM Mail exchange with employees and customers of that corporation worldwide;

As pressure for direct access to the wealth of information and personal contacts on the Internet increased during the early 1990s, the JANET management team initiated a project to develop a JANET IP Service (JIPS), to enable JANET sites to behave as though directly connected to the Internet network. This enabled sites to run the TCP/IP protocols necessary for interworking with Internet sites, through a so-called IP 'tunnel', by carrying IP traffic as X.25 data—in effect running one protocol on top of the other, disguised as data packets. Implicitly, this development has recognized the importance of TCP/IP at the present time for the research community, and recognizes the value in allowing the existence of alternative standard protocols on the same network for the benefit of global connectivity.

A JANET site must have the appropriate hardware—an IP router—and software installed to use the service, and must develop an Internet compatible naming scheme for directly linked users. Parallel running of protocols requires a user to launch the correct application for a particular need (and to know which this is), and so is not a transparent process to the user. For those with networking skills, however, the JIPS development opens out an enormously wider range of information and communication possibilities, and is a step within the UK towards greater international connectivity, as well as opening up access to more advanced information applications. A UK researcher can, from an office desktop, log in to the catalogue of the New York Public Library, retrieve copies of archived files from Sydney, and communicate with colleagues on the Pacific Rim, unconstrained by distance and time differences. By September 1992, over half the data traffic carried on JANET was IP traffic.

The introduction of multiple protocols does, however, introduce network management problems in relation to the end-user: everything must have two names—a JANET name and an Internet name and there are often duplicate applications for the same task, confusing the user. There are pressures within JANET to move to the use of the TCP/IP protocol suite as the underlying native mode, and it seems likely that this will occur in some parts, so that X.25 traffic is carried on top of an IP-based network, reversing the current position.

From 1993, parts of the JANET network are to be upgraded to a substantially higher speed and capacity in the SuperJANET project, to be installed by British Telecom. This project is intended to make use of advanced communications technology to provide research and education within the UK with a high speed, high performance broadband network capable of transmitting voice, data, and image together. This new network, using optical fibre, will upgrade the bandwidth available to a maximum of 140 Mbps using ATM packet switching techniques.

Working at a speed some 1000 times faster than the present JANET, this will enable the development of a range of applications and information services previously unfeasible. It is anticipated that early applications will include the use of distance learning courseware, electronic publishing, library document distribution, medical imaging, and multimedia information services.

The SuperJANET project intends to link into the existing Livenet network of the University of London, at present used to transmit live video images of medical surgery in operating theatres to classes of medical students, for teaching purposes. There is a two-way audio link with the theatre, so that students may ask questions of the surgeon, and an image base of still and video images as background material is also available. SuperJANET will extend this link to a wider audience of medical schools. Within the library field, a number of projects have been proposed, indicating a recognition of the importance of networking in this area.

1 Seven university libraries will co-operate in a resource sharing project on the delivery of journal articles in electronic form, with a much faster response than normal interlibrary loan methods.

2 A need has been identified amongst researchers who require access to high quality images of rare documentary material and archives, such as illustrated manuscripts, at different locations; a project will use ancient Persian manuscripts held at Manchester University to investigate this area.

3 A number of publishers are co-operating in the creation of a body of material to build an experimental electronic journal, covering a broad subject area which tests a variety of information needs—colour maps, graphics, half-tones, and scientific notation, for example.

The history of the JANET network shows that in a few short years, the available facilities are being used for applications never imagined in the early stages, and it is likely that a similar turn of events will overtake these initial ideas for SuperJANET. While it is certain that this round of development will result in unanticipated services as needs and understanding develop, it is less certain that the future funding and access mechanisms will remain as at present.

The Internet is an extensive academic and research-based network linking a very large number of broadly educational, research, and other related organizations across the United States and worldwide. It has a very large number of users and makes accessible a wide range of information services and resources. The Internet proper, in technical terms, refers to the relatively small number of machines which constitute nodes on the main network in the United States. Most people use the term, however, to refer to the vast range of networks, which may emanate from other countries as far apart as Canada, Israel, Germany, Mexico, New Zealand, and Australia. Within the United States, the enormous success of the Internet over the last five years is moving the network away from its beginnings as a traditional academic orientation towards a new and radical direction as a major national educational and community resource for economic development.

The Internet originally developed as a military network from projects funded by the Advanced Research Projects Agency of the US Department of Defence from 1969 onwards, and was known originally as ARPANET. In 1989, ARPANET was finally completely decommissioned from military service, and devoted to educational and research purposes. Along with other emerging state and national network elements, this began to become interlinked through a major data communications backbone established by the National Science Foundation between six new supercomputer sites in 1985. In the late 1980s, the National Science Foundation developed a high speed network backbone called *NSFnet* from the existing infrastructure, linking-some 16 main sites around the United States with data rates of 1.5 Mbits per second (known as the T1 standard).

The NSFnet forms the main data highway for the Internet, providing links via the 16 main sites to regional networks, and thence onwards to local networks and individual organizations. These main nodes may also provide gateways through to many other national and international networks, such as Earn (the European counterpart of BITNET) and CA net in Canada. The regional networks cover broad geographical areas, although with some overlap as a result of recent growth, and are run by a variety of organizations from commercial enterprises to government funded groups.

Parts of the NSFnet backbone are also provided by commercial enterprise, and this mix of public and private characterizes the Internet situation.

In principle, an organization which has an Internet connection, or 'feed', from a local or regional node, and which has the required equipment capacity, may itself provide any number of feeds to other organizations and individuals who are looking for an Internet account, relaying the network traffic back and forth on their behalf. In this way, the network is able to grow organically and, since one system user may have more than one feed available to it, can provide multiple communication pathways between sites, and therefore a more robust and reliable service.

By November 1992 nearly 8561 foreign, regional, state, and local networks constituted the Internet, connecting more than 700,000 host computers with an estimated 4 to 5 million users in 44 countries. In anticipation of serving a more widely expanded role, the NSFnet is currently being upgraded to support a much higher data transmission speed (45 Mbits per second, known as T3 standard), providing the bandwidth which will enable the development of a range of interactive services in multimedia telecommunications. This strengthened backbone is now referred to as a 'cloud' to emphasize its non-linear, interconnected, nature. The glue which binds all these diverse systems and machines together is the use of the TCP/IP communication protocols suite.

Most of the machines which constitute the Internet proper, and many of those which communicate with it, use this rather old, but widely used and constantly developing set of protocols; their widespread use in the Internet is part of its inheritance from the ARPANET, and is a major reason why TCP/IP usage is seen as the main rival to the open-systems movement.

Control of the network is distributed through various levels, with (at the moment) no overall control imposed from a central point. The main backbone NSFnet is currently managed by a not-for-profit consortium consisting of IBM, MCI (an important commercial network provider), and the Merit organization, based in Ann Arbor, Michigan.

The network uses a Domain Name System, similar to that of JANET, so that IP address numbers (long strings of digits) can be replaced by more explanatory structured domain names; the main difference from the JANET method is that these names are structured in reverse order, progressing from the narrower to the broader domain: from organization on the left to country on the right. New system users register with regional co-ordinators, who have the responsibility for mapping connection points, in order to make their existence known to other network users. This gives the Internet a much more informal flavour compared with JANET, making it difficult to say exactly how many Internet users exist, since there is no one point at which they are all counted.

There are agreed conventions on the use of the Internet to which all users are expected to conform: that it is intended for educational use and should not be used for purposes of commercial gain. This restriction is commonly quite broadly interpreted, and by no means all of the traffic between educational and other institutions is strictly educational in content; although it does preclude the offering of straightforward commercial services across the network, even though many organizations with Internet connections are commercial in nature. Some believe that this restriction will be relaxed in the near future.

The main decision-making body for the Internet is the

Internet Society, a voluntary organization which aims to promote Internet technology and developments. A sub-group of this, the Internet Architecture Board, is responsible for approving new and upgraded standards and for allocating resources such as IP addresses.

The Internet Engineering Task Force (IETF) is another voluntary body with open membership, which represents the user voice in Internet debates. The, IETF holds regular meetings—in Europe in 1993—and has a number of working groups developing specific issues. The Internet, then, depends to a large extent for its success on willing co-operation among its participants, and conformity to the spirit of network culture and etiquette. For example, an unwritten rule is that users who are established on the network through the benevolence of a host organization supplying their feed are ethically bound to consider similar requests made to them in the future. The cost of these connections is normally born as a part of the network overhead; by this means the overall cost is spread among the participants, so that network use often appears to the individual user as free, or at least providing unlimited usage for minimal cost.

There is a stronger tradition of more widespread public access to the Internet in the United States, with the availability of low cost dial-in lines as an alternative to full peer connection. Within the UK, there are a number of private organizations which provide Internet access as a commercial enterprise, for those who do not have an entree through the JANET network. This approach has been very successful, with a phenomenal growth in network activity from 1989 onwards, since when network traffic has grown, on average, by 20% per month. In the year up to October 1992, the total amount of network traffic in bytes almost doubled to about 3000 gigabytes per month. This phenomenal growth has catalysed the discussion on the future development of the Internet, and its methods of funding and management may change dramatically in the future.

Internet provides electronic mail services based on the Simple Mail Transfer Protocol (SMTP) mail convention. To a greater extent than in the UK, electronic mail has also given rise to a variety of alternative uses beyond the simple exchange of messages between individuals. A large number of news groups and discussion groups have grown up over the Internet based on the use of mail servers; within BITNET, which has become identical to the Internet for many practical purposes, these are known by the name of the listserv software used on IBM machines.

These function as automatic distribution lists for subscribers interested in an individual topic, which rebroadcast messages from individuals to the entire group. The Usenet newsgroups are also distributed over the Internet, and are available in a similar way. Listserver-type systems are present on numerous sites, rather than being centralized as in the UK Mailbase project, and there are hundreds of interest groups, ranging from technical discussions on aspects of computer science, through topics based on subject disciplines and educational and research issues, to social and recreational groups.

An example of one of the more active, for library and information workers, is PACS-L, dedicated to the discussion of public access computer systems; this has about 2000 members in several countries, and generates some 10-15 messages per day. Within the LIS field, there are groups centred around specific information service types, library systems suppliers, and broader social issues. There are estimated to be over 3500 conferences active, in addition to the Usenet newsgroups. Electronic mail is also used for the distribution of several electronic journals which are available over the Internet, most with free subscriptions. Once edited and compiled by human intervention, the journal may be distributed either in its entirety as a long e-mail message, or in the more sophisticated cases only as a contents page; subscribers can then receive individual articles as an e-mail message by sending a command which is automatically processed. Over 100 electronic journals, newsletters, and digests exist in the Internet environment. In this case, the listserver can be seen to function as a primitive database system. This practice saves on the use of network bandwidth by not transmitting unwanted information in the shape of unused articles; but also allows users to gather the information in the format most appropriate to their needs. Journals may also include graphics files, and text files may be available as plain ASCII or Postscript (laser printable) versions.

For sites with a direct Internet connection, real-time interactive access with public online information systems is available to remote sites. As with JANET, a common use is for access to online library catalogues. Since most of the main educational sites in the US are connected, a wide variety of catalogues are available, some with major collections—for example the Melvyl catalogue at the University of California, and that of the New York Public Library. An estimated 337 library catalogues are available through use of the Telnet remote access protocol. The Library of Congress files are accessible over the Internet, indicating the extent to which it is being used for formal purposes by library institutions. These files offer access to 28 million catalogue records included in the LCMARC files, together with copyright files, public policy citations and federal bill status files.

The Library also allows Internet access to its technical processing and cataloguing system, and to its SCORPIO reference and retrieval system. A wide spectrum of non-library sources of information are also available. Many of the government agencies attached to Internet make information resources openly available; these include, for instance, databases mounted by NASA in space science and astronomy and the CIA World Factbook. This kind of access is likely to increase in the future as the Internet develops: recent legislation colloquially known as the GPO Access Bill, for example, to require the US Government Printing Office to provide online public access to the Federal Register and the Congressional Record, as well as other material. A range of resources are listed in *The whole Internet* by Ed Kroll.

Sites with direct Internet access have the ability to transfer files directly from one machine to another in their original format, using the FTP protocol. The practice of 'anonymous ftp' has arisen in the Internet community, by which ftp archives are established on a host machine at a particular network site, with named directories which contain archives of files available for transfer.

Although computer system users would normally have to be registered with the site system administration in order to connect to a particular machine, these hosts have allowed free access to these specified ftp archives without the necessity to register a username or password beforehand; although it is normal practice to enter the caller's network address as the password information. This practice of 'anonymous ftp' is widely used to transfer entire documents, saving on the time-consuming necessity to view and save on-screen copies, and retaining any original formatting included with the file. The file can then be downloaded to a user's own machine, and used in whatever way is appropriate; the archive is able to distribute image as well as text-based information. Many ftp sites allow remote users to deposit files in the archive for others to retrieve.

A recent OCLC report estimated that there are about 3 million such files at more than a thousand ftp sites on the network, although the 20 largest sites account for more than half of these. Much of the material is source code for public domain computer programs, although the method is increasingly being used for the distribution of text files between specific groups or more widely. A major problem is that, as the report states 'the ability for network users to share information surpasses by far their ability to discover information on the Internet'.

As with JANET, a main problem with resources on the Internet lies in the difficulty of finding out what information is available. Since there is no central administration of the network which controls all uses of it, there is no central directory of resources, although distributed network information centres are emerging.

The problem is of a much greater magnitude than that faced by JANET, however, due to the much larger number of individual connections, and consequently the larger number of services and resources potentially available. It is also the case that resources are often duplicated in different network sites, and may exist in varying and incomplete versions and formats.

A number of resource guides have been drawn up by enthusiasts, covering both library-based databases, and those offered by other organizations, as well as lists of discussion and news groups which are known to exist; some of these documents are listed in Appendix B. These text documents may themselves be available in ftp archives, or retrievable as mail messages. None of these, however, is fully comprehensive, and all are subject to swift outdating in the climate of rapid change.

Long-term answers to the problem are the subject of debate, especially among some sections of the library community.

From 1992, the Internet is poised on the brink of a further phase of development. A concept sponsored by Vice-President Albert Gore for many years, and now enacted in the High Performance Computing Act of 1991, promises to continue national development in the existing interconnected array of networks to upgrade and expand the system, opening it out to more colleges, schools, and public libraries as a national research and educational resource. This 'information superhighway', to be known as the National Research and Education Network (NREN), will aim for the development of a national 3 gigabit per second (a gigabit = one thousand million bits of data) network capacity by 1996. This represents an increase of approximately 2000 times over the current bandwidth, and as a rough guide would make the network capable of carrying 100,000 pages of text or 1000 bit-mapped photographic images each second.

As with SuperJANET, this will support a vast expansion in the number and range of services possible, and make multimedia communications such as desktop videoconferencing feasible as an everyday reality. Another major goal for NREN is the standardization of protocols across the existing patchwork of networks, and the integration of TCP/IP with OSI protocols to enable both to be used in parallel. This is not an isolated development, but is indicative of a number of initiatives within this vein in the United States.

The Pacific Bell corporation, for example, is building a broadband network (CalREN) in California to link participating universities, research laboratories, major hospitals, and leading high technology firms in the Los Angeles and Bay Area to develop innovative applications for education, healthcare, and business. These include projects such as the use of tele-seminars for remote educational programmes, medical image processing, remote patient monitoring, and specialist diagnosis, and the development of collaborative precompetitive research with industry and commerce.

Proponents of the NREN argue that the United States is falling behind in economic competitiveness because government, business, industry, and education cannot access the information resources which it needs to maintain international competitiveness and economic strength. Another school of thought argues that such needs would be best met by market forces in the shape of existing commercial networks such as MCI, funded by charging market prices for services. This argument has raised serious issues on future policies for the NREN on the issue of charging of services, which at the moment appear as though free to many end-users; and the use of NREN by commercial service providers.

Campus wide information systems

As the wider area networking scene has been undergoing substantial development, the local focus of higher educational networking has also seen significant developments. Concepts such as the 'electronic library', in which larger proportions of educational support material are delivered in electronic form to users who are more geographically dispersed, have raised the profile of local networking as a means of integrating access to the diverse range and types of information available from all sources within the campus environment. In recent years, such developments have been carried out under the name of campus-wide information systems (CWIS), which are intended to bring together this variety of local information within a single framework.

Access to this information should be simplified by an easy to use interface, which does not present barriers to the casual user, and is potentially available from all points of the local network. In many ways, this parallels some of the forms of community information systems which have emerged as civic facilities, but is more localized upon and targeted at a smaller and more easily identifiable community. The concept of a CWIS as a broad umbrella encompassing diverse information types precludes too strict a set of conditions on the structure and format of the information; in this sense, the CWIS forms an information base of both structured and less structured information, rather than a database in the precise sense of the term. A typical CWIS might include:

- — staff and student directory information, including telephone, postal and e-mail addresses;
- — a diary of local events and university calendars;
- — course information, administrative details and timetables;
- — a listing of research projects and interests;
- — university rules and regulations;
- — newsletters related to the local campus;
- — community and travel information;
- — library catalogues and library service information;
- — locally produced indexes and databases;
- — links to other CWIS, catalogues etc., located at different campuses.

By bringing this information together in one access structure, a CWIS can help to integrate a campus community which is split between different sites or spread over a wide area and develop a sense of community. There is also some interest in developing this approach as a method for inter-university communication at the campus level to encourage collaborative endeavours and cooperation, rather than through formal administrative structures. There are about 20 different campus wide information systems in the UK at the present time, although these can take very different forms, and a formal categorization is difficult; and there seems to be extensive interest in exploring the potential of the idea further.

The information system can be developed as an extension of a library online catalogue, and be included within the same framework as an available network resource, or be developed as a general computer-support facility. The direction from which the impetus for development comes is likely to influence the shape of the outcome, and the underlying objectives it is intended to achieve.

The CWIS may be centralized onto a single machine from which remote access is possible, or act as a gateway to other local systems, calling the information up as needed. Whether the CWIS takes a centralized or more distributed approach, the task of maintaining and updating the information is normally the responsibility of the information providers. This may be either by submitting updated files to the operators of a centralized system, or by directly maintaining the data in one of the nodes which constitute a distributed system, to which the CWIS offers gatewayed access. In either case, the CWIS is essentially acting as a framework for the presentation of data, rather than determining the content too precisely.

13

Computers in Schools

George Mamunes, 14, a gangling ninth-grader dressed in flannel shirt, blue jeans and hiking boots, knits his thick, dark eyebrows while putting the finishing touches on a computer program, already nearly 300 lines long. For those uninitiated in the special languages of the computer age, it looks like a hopeless mess of numerical gibberish.

The electronic heart is part of a teaching tool George is putting together for eighth-grade biology classes. A few feet away sits Pam Miller, 14, a ninth-grader with long, brown hair draped far down her back. She is operating a computer program—or software—that simulates the workings of a nuclear reactor. Today she is fine-tuning the section that governs the control rods, those regulators of the reactor's nuclear fires. Tapping away at the keyboard, Pam explains: "You have to maximize the power output without destroying the reactor." Suddenly, flashing numbers burst upon the screen. "There," says Pam, her face lighting up. "Reactor overheated. Power output low. Reactor core damaged. Melt-down!" A disaster that she has brought on intentionally, just to show how it could happen.

Other disciples, seated at terminals scattered around the room, are no less absorbed. Meilin Wong, 15, chic in blue velour blouse, jeans and Bass moccasins, is trying to figure out what went wrong with her business data management program. She is an old hand at such troubleshooting, having spent much of last semester "debugging" a program that, when printed-out, stretches over 30 ft. Jim McGuire, 13, is creating a video game called Spaceship, which will let electronic star warriors zap a boxy-looking orbital intruder.

A more mundane program is emerging from 15-year -old Dave McCann's terminal: a verb test for seventh- and eighth-grade Spanish classes. Off in a corner two youngsters are putting the impish face of Mad magazine's cartoon hero, Alfred E. Neuman, onto the computer screen. Says Muller, as he presides proudly over these after-hours computer converts: "No one told them they have to be here. They're not usually doing assignments. They're experimenting. They're letting their imaginations run free." *t*-Muller's disciples are not all math whizzes. Or straight-A students. Or particularly precocious. They are reasonably normal youngsters who have grown up with computers. For them, in ways that few people over 30 can understand, manipulating these complex machines is as natural as riding a bike, playing baseball or even solving Rubik's cube. Like thousands of others across the country, they are part of a revolutionary vanguard: the computer generation. Not only is this generation propelling traditional education down promising avenues, it is tugging at the entire social fabric, foreshadowing changes at least as startling and momentous as those ushered in by a new generation of automobile users more than a half-century ago.

In the classroom, where youngsters are being introduced to the machines as early as kindergarten, they astound—and often outpace—their teachers with their computer skills. After school they gather at the mushrooming number of computer stores (more than 1500 at last count) or join the computer clubs that are becoming a regular part of the youthful landscape. Huddling around any available machine, they argue over their programs, thresh out computer problems and swap software as intensely as kids once haggled over baseball cards.

In the summer, they may even go off to computer camps, another growth industry, and if they are Boy Scouts, they may try for a computer merit badge. During mischievous moments, they may tinker with one another's programs, writing in steps that will flash an unexpected insult or obscenity across a buddy's video screen. Some try to pick the encoded electronic locks on copyrighted software, taking glee in outwitting their elders, or spin fanciful plots to break into computer networks.

A few turn their skills to profit by showing baffled businessmen how to get idle, new computers to run, or by establishing Delaware-based corporations to market their own software creations. To the bafflement of their parents, they talk in a jargon of their own ("Hey, Charlie, you should have POKED instead of PEEKED"). As with so many other changes in contemporary life, the spark for this revolution is technological: a bit of silicon sophistication variously known as the personal, home or microcomputer. No larger than an attache case, apart from its video screen, this mighty mite packs the computing power of machines that two decades ago occupied a full room. Yet the micros, as they are affectionately called, are a relative bargain to buy and are becoming steadily cheaper.

Many models cost under $1000, bringing them

within reach of schools, parents or the children themselves. Last week, in the sharpest price break yet, Timex announced it will begin selling a small home computer for a suggested retail price of $99.95. But size and price cannot explain why computers have taken such a strong hold on so many youngsters. Certainly their interest has been stirred by a related rage, video games, whose computer-generated flashes, zaps, and pings have not only all the appeal pinball machines had for their elders but go a significant step further: they pique young minds to learn more about all that electronic prestidigitation. But many experts, and most of the young operatives, agree that the overwhelming attraction of the machines is the lure of control, the pleasure of being able to think out and then make something happen, a satisfaction all too often denied children.

Recognized by students and teachers alike as his school's best computer programmer, Lewis works afternoons as an instructor for a computer consulting firm, introducing younger children to the machines. Last year his employers sent him to Chicago, where he displayed his special teaching gifts before a meeting of educators. As Lewis told *Time* correspondent Peter Stoler, "we love these machines. I've got all this power at my fingertips. Without computers, we don't know what do be. With them, I'm somebody."

Perhaps because of the faintly macho side of computers, the bug seems to strike many more boys than girls in the pre-adolescent years. Says Steve Siegelbaum, Lewis's teacher: "Maybe it's because boys are pushed more toward math and logic than girls are. Maybe it's because boys are just more aggressive." Paradoxically, the computer passion is often stirred in youngsters who seem least likely to be interested in high tech. Jay Harstad, 12, of Minnetonka, Minn., litters his house with poems and sketches but will do almost anything to avoid doing his math homework. Yet Jay is one of the Gatewood Elementary School's premier computerniks and regularly helps teachers introduce fourth-graders to the machines. At West High School in Wausau, Wis., Chris Schumann, 16, a junior, has made a name for himself by translating musical notes into digital form and getting a computer to play Bach and Vivaldi through its loudspeaker. Originally, Chris regarded computers as remote and forbidding, but that changed when he was introduced to his first micro. "It looked real friendly," he says. "It didn't overpower you. It wasn't this ominous thing but something you could get close to."

The closeness can be contagious. Explains Nick Newman, 15, Muller's chief disciple at Ridgewood: "The more you do on the machine, the more enjoyable it gets. It becomes habit-forming." In Alpena, Mich., youngsters who had learned computer skills in junior high were devastated when they got to senior high school and found too few machines to go around. Says Alpena Elementary School principal Burt Wright: "I've got high school kids begging to come in after school and use our machine." The truly addicted—known half scornfully, half admiringly as computer nerds—may drop out almost entirely from the everyday world. In Lexington, Mass., one legendary 16-year-old nerd got so deeply immersed in computers that he talked to no one, headed straight to his terminal after school and barely sat down for meals.

The only way his father could get him away from the terminal was to go down to the cellar and throw the house's main power switch, cutting off all electricity. Barry Porter, 14, of San Francisco, is a computer-age truant, so attached to the machine that he often skips school, rarely reads anything other than computer manuals and hangs out with his pals in the Market Street computer store, often plotting some new electronic scam. Barry (not his real name) currently boasts an illicit library of about 1000 pirated (*i.e.* illegally copied) programs worth about $50,000 at retail prices, including such software gems as VisiCalc, the popular business management and planning program. Before security was tightened up, he regularly plugged his computer into such distant databanks as the Source (which provides news bulletins, stock prices, etc.) via telephone without paying a cent.

No one can say exactly when the computer generation began—certainly not earlier than the 1960s, when computers began appearing in schools. But even computer whizzes in their twenties are acutely aware of how soon they are likely to be outstripped by today's grade schoolers. Says Steven jobs, 27, the multimillionaire co-founder of Apple Computer Inc.: "These kids know more about the new software than we do." New York computer executive Charles Lecht goes further: "If you were born before 1965, boy, you're going to be out of it." Where their parents fear to tread, the microkids plunge right in, no more worried about pushing incorrect buttons or making errors than adults are about dialling a wrong telephone number. Says mathematician Louis Robinson, IBM's resident computer sage: "They know what computers can and cannot do, while adults still regard them as omnipotent." Says Hughes Aircraft Chairman Allen Puckett, who shares an Apple with son Jim, 12: "A lot of adults grew up in a slide-rule world and still reject computers. But computers are as natural to kids as milk and cookies."

More and more members of the computer generation are tasting the heady pleasure of teaching their own teachers how to use the machines and, if they are lucky enough to have computers at home, instructing their parents as well. Says Ridgewood's Newman, a regular teacher of teachers: "It's a sort of mutual doorway. The barriers between adult and child, between teacher and student, are broken, and it's person to person. Nobody's looking down on anyone; they're looking each other right in the eye." Often adults find it easier to ask a child how to do something than to ask another adult. Says University of Kansas education professor Mary Kay Corbitt: "One adult student of mine brought her son to computer class, and we discovered that he was doing her assignment while she watched. Two weeks later she overcame her anxieties and was participating fully." Confronted with the strange and unsettling world of the computer, teachers can get a useful perspective on what it is like to be a student again. After taking part in an elementary course in programming, Lois Brown, 54, a Wausau grade-school teacher, is thoroughly chastened. "Now we realize how little kids feel when there's a concept they don't understand. We sat in that course not wanting anyone to know all the things we didn't understand." Despite their obvious wariness of computers, parents are taking the lead in getting them into the schools. In Florida, communities have staged cake and candy sales, carnivals and tree plantings, weekend car washes, even a bike-a-thon to raise funds to buy computers. Says Marilyn Neff of Miami: "We feel computers will be the new paper and pencil." Of the 250 computers in the schools of Utica, Mich., more than two-thirds have been purchased by parent-sponsored fund drives. Says Utica Principal Paul Yelinsky: "Moms and dads are coming in and telling the counsellors they have to get their kids in computer classes because it's the wave of the future." So important is computer literacy that the Alfred P. Sloan Foundation is beginning a major program to get even such traditional liberal arts schools as St John's College in Maryland to begin giving courses in it. Though many schools began purchasing computers with federal aid budget cutbacks are drying up that well. Apple's jobs points out that other nations, especially Britain, France and the Soviet Union—though surprisingly not the electronics-minded Japanese—are paying far more attention to computer education than is the US. Earlier this year, jobs persuaded California Congressman Pete Stark and Missouri Senator John Danforth to introduce bills in Congress that would allow computer manufacturers to take a hefty tax write-off for any machines they donate to elementary and high schools. Under the present law, full deductions for such scientific equipment are allowed only if it is given to colleges and universities.

Jobs originally spoke of giving an Apple to every public elementary and secondary school in the country, more than 80,000 computers worth as much as $200 million retail. Now he thinks private schools should be included and is encouraging other manufacturers to join in the program as well. Meanwhile, Apple's archrival, the Tandy Corp., maker of the Radio Shack computer line, is taking a different tack: it has pledged $500,000 in equipment to spur development of educational programming, or courseware, for the classroom. Many of the approximately 100,000 computers now in US schools—roughly one for every 400 students—are in affluent suburbs like Ridgewood, a national leader in computer education. But the machines are also found in the unlikeliest of places. On a Chippewa Indian reservation in Wisconsin, computers are being used by young members of the tribe to learn their ancient and nearly forgotten language. Alaska's small rural schools have been ordering computers to meet a special need: they allow students of different ages and abilities in the same small classrooms to learn at their own pace. Dubuque, Iowa, where the *New Yorker* founding editor

Harold Ross disdainfully located his provincial old lady, has 13 machines and another 20 on order. Bill Holloway, a professor of computer education at the University of Kansas, calls the spread of small computers in the classroom nothing less than an avalanche. According to various industry studies, there may be from 300,000 to 650,000 computers in the schools by 1985.

So far, the most common, and least interesting, way to use school computers is in direct drill and review. The machine simply quizzes, prods and grades the student, very much like a robot teacher. Hundreds of programs of this type are available for popular computers like the Apple II Plus, Radio Shack's TRS-80 and the Commodore PET. But many of these programs are little more than computerized rehashes of the old classroom flash cards that go back to the days of McGuffey's readers. One notable difference: today when the student answers correctly, the screen will light up with WOWS, HOORAYS or smiling animals. Wrong answers may produce sad or scowling faces, perhaps accompanied by a falling tear. Partly because of teachers' fears—of the machines and for their jobs—and partly because of the poor quality of software, the frequently heralded electronic revolution in the classroom has been slow to occur. Now, however, it is being pushed along by steady improvements in teaching programs, thanks to imaginative enterprises like the Minnesota Educational Computing Consortium.

One of its more refreshing drills: a program called Wrong Note, which helps teach sight reading of musical scores. As a simple tune emanates from the computer's loudspeaker, matching notes appear on the screen, but sometimes the quiz intentionally errs and obliges students to find the false note. In order to do so, they can order up a repetition of the tune as often as Bogie and company did in *Casablanca.* Says Kenneth Brumbaugh, director of the consortium's instructional services: "Imagine asking a teacher to play it again and again!" Even very young children can profit from such exercises. At the Nordstom Elementary School in Morgan Hill, Calif., a suburb of San Jose, Colin Devenish, 7, is working with a classmate on the arithmetic drill, honing his skills in addition and subtraction. Unlike youngsters doing such drilling in the past, Colin seems to be enjoying himself enormously. Why? "Because," he replies mischievously within earshot of his teacher, "the computer doesn't yell."

Computers, operated only by touching a few buttons, are also remarkably effective devices for educating the handicapped. At the California School for the Deaf in Fremont, Rhonda Revera, 16, has worked with computers for five years, studying every subject from fractions to spelling. Rhonda offers a paean to the machine in sign language: "Computer makes me remember. It is fast, easy and better than writing on paper." Still another important use of computers is as a remedial tool. One is a spelling drill with a special incentive built into it: if all the answers are correct, a video game pops onto the screen as a reward. When one youngster worked his way through the drill, even classroom hecklers were impressed. Said one: "Hey, Old Wentworth's getting better." More entertaining and demanding are think tank-type strategy games like Geography Search, which launches competing teams on a Columbus-like voyage of exploration. They must make their way across the Atlantic, taking into account currents and winds, finding their longitude and latitude by means of star patterns and the length of a shadow thrown by a stick at high noon (methods that worked for Columbus, after all), and coping with such unforeseen perils as an outbreak of scurvy, an attack by pirates and a tropical storm. Only shrewd planning, wise choices and cooperative action ensure survival. The simulated voyage becomes uncannily real to the participants. Says the game's creator, Thomas Snyder, 31, who heads Computer Learning Connection, Inc., of Cambridge, Mass.: "When they get near the end and the computer finally shows them another ship near by, they act as if they had actually spotted a ship at sea."

Until a few years ago, the few computers available in secondary schools were essentially "dumb" terminals linked by telephone lines to a large, centrally located machine that served a variety of users through an arrangement called time-sharing. All the courseware was stored in the big computer's powerful memory, which could be tapped at will by students and teachers. The most successful example of such a system—and the one still used by Wisconsin's Chippewa Indians—is PLATO (for Programmed Logic for Automatic Teaching Operations).

Developed in the 1960s by the University of Illinois and Control Data Corp., PLATO is an exemplary teacher containing more than 8000 hours of courseware, much of it in a continuous curriculum. Thus, if a youngster forgets a point from an earlier lesson, PLATO will search its prodigious memory and patiently recapitulate. But such time-sharing schemes are extremely expensive, since they require open lines to the central computer. They also can become backed up at peak hours, and do not always lend themselves readily to what is the most intellectually demanding use of the computer: learning how to program it. For this, the inexpensive, easy-to-operate personal computer, entirely self-contained and relying on equipment immediately at the student's side, is an ideal instrument—much more "user-friendly," as manufacturers like to say, than big machines. Yet even with a handy micro, programming can overwhelm the uninitiated. The programmer and computer must "speak" a common language. In the early days of the digital computer, this was extremely difficult.

The machine reduces all the information it receives, whether it arrives as letters, numbers or graphic symbols, into the simplest possible electronic statements: either a yes or a no, represented by pulses of high or low voltage. To command the machine in its own internal language meant writing out endless strings of one or zeros, called bits and bytes, symbolizing those yes or no statements. But scientists soon began creating alternate languages for communicating with the machines that vaguely resemble everyday speech. The most popular of these computer tongues is BASIC (for Beginner's All-purpose Symbolic Instruction Code).

Developed at Dartmouth by mathematician John Kemeny and his colleague Thomas Kurtz to let even the least mathematically gifted student converse with the university's computers, it is "understood" by virtually all of today's personal computers. To show just how easy the language is, Kemeny offers this extremely simple lesson in programming: tell the computer to find the square roots (i.e., the numbers that, when multiplied by themselves, yield the original numbers) of eleven successive values, say 20 through 30.

The entire operation can be accomplished for a program of just four steps:

```
1  FOR N = 20 TO 30

2  PRINT N, SQR(N)

3  NEXT N

4  END
```

Translated into everyday language, the first line tells the computer to let N stand successively for 20 through 30.

The second instructs the machine to print the first value of N (that is, the number 20), compute its square root (SQR) and print out the result. The third tells the computer to go on to each of the succeeding values all the way through 30. Finally, the program tells the computer to call it a day, its job having been done. Even the smallest machine can do such calculations in a flash, compared with the hours of work they might require of human computers. To preserve their creativity, the students can readily store their programs on magnetic tape or on a small, 45 rpm-size plastic record called a floppy disc—which is not, as some parents believe, a new form of back injury. Then when the occasion arises for using the program again, the computer operator merely loads the instructions back into the machine and punches in some new values for N.

The same broad principles apply to the creation of all software, even complex simulations like Geography Search. Literal-minded brutes that they are, computers do exactly what they are told. No more and no less. But youngsters of even the most tender age are surprising educators by showing they can master the beasts with startling ease. Computer software expert Leona Schauble of the Children's Television Workshop (producers of *Sesame Street)* recalls getting an eight-year-old boy at Manhattan's Little Red School House started on a simple computer game.

The game generated an image of a frog that would leap up and catch a butterfly, provided the right buttons were hit. After a few minutes, she checked back and found the frog jumping in slow motion. When she asked the youngster what happened, he replied, "Well, we wanted to make the frog catch more butterflies. So we got a listing of the variables and slowed him down." In other words, the youngster had broken into the game's program and changed it to suit himself.

To instruct very young children, even Kemeny's BASIC is much too mathematical. Instead, more and more schools are turning to an innovative computer language called LOGO (from the Greek word for reason), developed by Seymour Papert and his colleagues at MIT. A mathematician who studied with the Swiss psychologist jean Piaget, Papert has become something of a guru of the computer generation, predicting that the machines will revolutionize learning by taking much of the mystery out of mathematics, science and technology. Says he: "The computer can make the most abstract things concrete."

With a deceptively simple set of commands, LOGO enables youngsters who know nothing of geometry and algebra, and barely know how to read, to manipulate a triangular figure, dubbed the Turtle, on a computer screen and trace all manner of shapes with it. At the Lamplighter School in Dallas, teachers using LOGO get youngsters of three or four to write simple computer instructions. In one game, they maneuver "cars" and "garages" on the computer screen in such a way that the cars are parked inside the garages. While playing with LOGO, the youngsters learn simple words, the difference between left and right, and geometric concepts that they would not ordinarily encounter until junior high.

The machines crop up in the lives of youngsters even before they enter school—and sometimes before they learn to walk or talk—in the guise of such siliconised gadgetry as Little Professor and Speak & Spell. With a few presses of the button, these computerized games produce flashing lights, squealing sounds and disembodied voices that inculcate the rudiments of spelling and calculating. A record of sorts may have been set by Corey Schou, a computer scientist at the University of Central Florida in Orlando: he rigged up a home computer so his five-month-old daughter could operate it by pressing buttons in her crib and changing the designs on a nearby screen. Says the proud papa: "Basically, it's an electronic kaleidoscope, another diversion, another learning device." Whatever it is, it prepares youngsters for all those buttons they will encounter soon enough in and out of school. Parents and teachers may shudder at the thought, but it is only a short hop from skilful operation of a video game to learning fundamentals of programming. Says MIT Sociologist Sherry Turkle, 33, who has been studying the youthful computer culture for five years: "The line between game playing and programming is very thin. Programming takes what is powerful about games—this articulation of knowledge, this learning about strategy—and carries it to a higher level of power." By the time the youthful programmers reach the eighth or ninth grade, their skills may reach a marketable level. In Chicago, Jonathan Dubman, 14, and Kay Borzsony, 13, have formed a company called Aristotle Software to sell their own computer games and graphics programs. Says Kay: "The nice thing about the computer business is that there is no real bias against children. In the computer magazines, you read articles by 12- and 13-year-olds." Laura Hyatt, 15, of Ridgewood, helps a stymied local insurance office figure out how to use its software. Says she: "It's better than babysitting." And, at $3.50 an hour, somewhat more profitable.

The prodigy of prodigies may be Eugene Volokh, 14, of Los Angeles. A Russian emigre, he earns $480 each week by doing 24 hours of programming for 20th Century-Fox, while carrying a full load of courses as a junior at UCLA. This year Greg Christensen, 18, of Anaheim, Calif., could make $100,000 in royalties from a video game he developed that was bought by Atari. Other youngsters are waiting at the sidelines in hopes of catching up with these young entrepreneurs. Every Tuesday night, Scott Whitfield, 13, and his brother Shawn, 11, appear at the Menlo Park, Calif., public library to get computer instruction. Says Scott: "We'll probably never get a job if we don't learn how to use a computer." Not all youngsters take equally to the machines. In a typical computer class, only about one in five students becomes seriously involved. Says Steven Scott, 16, of Wausau's West High: "Either you get the hang of it or you don't." Even so dedicated a computernik as Ridgewood's Nick Newman finds programming interesting only for a purpose. His own goal is to apply his computer knowledge to a career in science or medicine. Whatever these youngsters make of their computer experiences, they will surely confront the world differently from their parents.

The precise, orderly steps of logic required to use and program the machines promise to shape—and sharpen—the thought processes of the computer generation. Indeed, the youngsters playing all those strategy games are doing precisely what corporations do when they plan to launch a new product, or what military leaders do when they devise strategies to confront a potential foe. Whether such abilities will change the world for the better is another matter. Princeton psychologist George Miller, for one, has doubts that "a few years of thinking like a computer can change patterns of irrational thought that have persisted throughout recorded history."

Other social critics ask if clear thinking is enough—if, in fact, there might not be a danger in raising a generation to believe that it has the analytical tools to contemplate any problem. Says MIT computer science professor Joseph Weizenbaum: "There's a whole world of real problems, of human problems, which is essentially being ignored." It is still impossible, after all, to reduce a human relationship to a printout or to solve a moral question by bits and bytes.

Some critics predict a future not unlike that portrayed in Isaac Asimov's I, *Robot,* a science fiction novel set in a society so thoroughly computer-dominated that the people cannot do arithmetic. Humanist critic George Steiner acerbically calls the computer generation the advance guard of a breed of "computer-mutants." Says Steiner: "They will be out of touch with certain springs of human identity and creativity, which belong to the full use of language rather than mathematical and symbolical codes."

Many others are much more sanguine. University of Chicago philosopher of science Stephen Toulmin predicts that computers will "re-intellectualize" the television generation. "TV relieved people of the necessity to do anything," says Toulmin. "Computers depend on what you do yourself." Catholic theologian David Tracy argues that "using computers sharpens the mind's ability to deal with our world: the world of technology." The final word may be simpler, and not pronounced by elders who find a devilish soul in the new machine. More so than adults, the young know the computer for what it is. Says a 10-year-old at Manhattan's Bank Street School: "It's dumb. We have to tell it everything." They also know something important is afoot. Says Shawn Whitfield: "When I grow up it's going to be the Computer Age.

14

Future of Networking

A major development in the short- to medium-term future will be a substantial growth in multimedia telecommunications in one form or another. In this way, multimedia information networks will correspond more closely to the experience of communication and information interchange in everyday life, with a flexible mix of sound, picture, and words. The exact nature of this experience, and its effect on information networking in general, remains to be determined.

A major preoccupation of national governments and regional associations is to build the infrastructure for these developments as quickly as possible (and preferably faster than their competitors). In the United States, for example, in an attempt to accelerate the extension of fibre optic cabling to the home and workplace on a massive scale, the Federal Communications Commission (FCC) decided in 1992 to allow the regional Bell holding companies to transmit video programmes over their telecommunications lines, in competition with the cable television companies. This attempt to create a communications infrastructure for the next decade is seen by many Americans as crucial to the continued economic dominance of the United States.

The FCC, for example, places much weight on multimedia devices such as high definition television (HDTV), a digital two-way interactive television set, as the vehicle for this information expansion, aiming at a 15-year deadline for complete HDTV conversion. The technological futurism is the subject of much political controversy and manoeuvring at the current time; it seems likely though, that the new presidential administration will lead out more liberalization to support competition-led innovation and technological advances in communications media, and there is a clear emphasis on the use of technology for economic development in the shaping of public policy statements.

One more immediate result is likely to be the more rapid development of the National Research and Education Network, sponsored for many years by Vice-President Al Gore. The building of NREN services will bring into focus many of the issues on information access and price, and of the emerging adjustments in role of all those involved in the information cycle. In Europe, a similar urgency has fuelled a number of projects sponsored by the European Commission to work towards the creation of integrated broadband communications systems by the latter part of this decade.

The RACE programme, funding research into advanced communications technology and services, indicates by its name some of its underlying objectives, and the ESPRIT programme has initiated the IDOMENEUS project to co-ordinate and improve European efforts in the development of new information environments in the area of interacting open media.

Adopting lessons learned from the French experience in the establishment of the Minitel system, the

EC has initiated a number of pilot projects in fields ranging from banking and finance, manufacturing, transport, distribution, and health care; other projects include distributed multimedia publishing, and a broadband network based library for the petroleum and chemical industries, with a 1995 target date for the introduction of commercial services.

The existence of a technology, however, does not always guarantee its success. It is worth remembering that the Picture Phone was launched by AT&T at the World Fair of 1964. This was a first example of the videophone; in 1992, almost 30 years later, British Telecom launched a low-cost consumer videophone, which can be connected directly to the normal telephone socket; this has yet to make any substantial impact in the market-place.

A development which is likely to be of more significance, though, is the planned availability of audio-visual workstations based on the standard PC. Such a device will make the full integration of data and voice networks within the workplace a reality, and will open up a wider market for multimedia information services. Many of these exist in prototype form within the existing infrastructure, Multimedia electronic mail, for example, is now possible even in a limited text-based medium such as the Internet.

The multimedia information mail extensions (MIME) to the standard Internet mail protocol permit the inclusion of still images, group III fax images, compressed full motion video, and multipart playback sequences of mixed information types. Desktop videoconferencing, the ability to conduct meetings with a geographically remote person each at their own desk, has been established as a feasible communications technology, although so far finding only a niche rather than global market. The experience of this videoconferencing raises some key issues since it is clear that, as with most other information technologies, the technical issues are much less important than the social and organisational ones. Technical advances which have made the idea more feasible include the emergence of high bandwidth ISDN networks, video compression techniques, accepted standards, and powerful graphics-based workstations.

The degree of success in implementing this technology is determined rather by the extent to which it supports the way people work. The involves an understanding of the communications patterns between individuals and groups, and of their information needs and the uses to which information is put; of the way in which contacts with individuals and formal information sources assists the innovative process, and an appreciation of the interdependent balance between formal and informal communication.

Technology has often been used to support formal communication patterns, rather than the informal, and sometimes is intended to replace rather than support either. Multimedia communications systems cannot replace face-to-face contact any more than the telephone (although a similar argument was made against the telephone at its introduction). Thoughtful design may, however, be used to appropriately support existing human communication patterns. The Cruiser videoconferencing system designed by Bellcore, for example, uses the metaphor of a 'virtual hallway'—floor plan representing the groups of participants—along which a user may navigate, 'cruise' and interact with others in the process. For multimedia multi-user systems such as this, the interface must include some form of social protocol which enables decisions about the nature and style of desired interaction to be taken.

Many issues which will effectively delineate the shape of multimedia networking in the future remain as yet poorly understood and little explored. In some areas, however, there is more immediacy on concerns which are being raised by the substantial growth in network traffic and users, and the potential changes which can be perceived in the near future.

The growing importance of digital information and its availability over networks which demand physical and technical access create barriers which are increasingly insurmountable for many groups of potential users. While there is no space here to discuss the social role of information systems, there are a few examples of attempts to bypass these barriers in recent developments. The Cleveland FreeNet experiment, for example, is an attempt to increase access to Internet information to a wider audience. The vast amounts of information, and the worldwide nature of the Internet, also bring to the fore issues of intellectual property and copyright surrounding electronic information. Much of the information held on this network is freely available, as long as it is used for non-commercial purposes.

The subsequent use of information taken from computer networks cannot be controlled, however, once it has been downloaded from the original source. It may appear in many diverse guises, be re-partitioned, amalgamated, and reused, taking on a life of its own. Print-based copyright legislation does not translate easily to the electronic environment. A feature of the legislation to found the advanced NREN network requires the provision of charging mechanisms to be put in place, suggesting a trend towards more control over use and users.

The characteristics which make electronic information difficult to define and 'freeze' at one point in time also raise questions on the nature of bibliographic control and mapping of information resources. Electronic documents and journals which can be updated immediately, replacing the original copy, are difficult to define as a bibliographic entity which has a declared and fixed content, which can be cited for later use. The identification of various versions of a logical item becomes a complex (or perhaps impossible) task, as does preservation and archiving as a permanent record of publication. These problems also redound upon ethical issues involving the quality and accuracy of the document content. Electronic documents may easily be changed, or 'falsified' with changing intellectual fashions in a way that print fixed at one point in time cannot.

The unstructured and fluid process which allows a network user to make information available without recourse to formal publisher or refereeing process has great advantages in stimulating an innovative and creative dialectic, but at the cost of a large proportion of false, misleading, or incorrect information which must also be sorted through and rejected. Whilst the research community, in which much of this type of activity takes place at present, has evolved a fairly sophisticated code of practical ethics for network co-operation and exchange, it is doubtful that this will survive a broadening of access and the introduction of commercial interests.

The increasing ubiquity of the networking environment is raising questions about the relative responsibilities of those involved in the information transfer process. Traditionally, this process could be described in terms of five distinct roles: the information provider, who provides the original source material; the information host, who makes it available and accessible, 'publishing' in a print or electronic sense; the carrier or distributor, providing a channel for the information; the intermediary, traditional role for the information service professional; and the information user, the final consumer. This model has long ago begun to break down when applied to the networking environment.

The information provider is often the same as the information host; the common carrier, the telecommunications authority, provides information services in its own right; and the information user more often wishes to find and retrieve the information directly. Many people have begun to question the role of the publisher in the electronic environment: since the author can mount a document in its electronic form on a local computer (quite probably the format it was originally composed in) and the network facilities act as a distribution mechanism, it becomes harder to gauge the function of a traditional publisher. Although this is clearly not appropriate for many types of publishing, in some areas it is possible to see advantages.

For instance, the traditional venue for reporting research has been as a journal article in some summarized form; network publishing would allow a reader to optionally download original datasets and intermediate analysis, as well as authorial commentary, directly and without a time delay. The development of network publishing is likely to involve identifiable changing characteristics compared to the traditional activities:

— a growth in simulcast publishing, with one source file producing a variety of complementary versions in different formats;

— multimedia electronic publishing, integrating database, text, image, sound, and video;

— the use of information tools to skim, navigate, browse, and utilize these new media products;

— selective and customized publishing targeted at particular groups;
— a linking with the concept of a 'virtual library', where access and materials are not constrained by physical barriers.

The information user and the information provider potentially have a much more direct and interactive relationship, possibly to the extent that the information exchange cannot be completely separated from the communication process itself. This raises a question mark against the received role of the intermediary, as a filter between originator, distributor, and recipient.

As the growth in electronic information begins to demand a new philosophy of the nature and function of information so also the activities of the information professional must, in this setting at least, change and adapt. No longer able to adopt a custodial role in managing and organizing the materials and artefacts of information, the librarian or information scientist must adopt a facilitating strategy, aimed at creating the conditions for a user to negotiate the information sphere successfully. The librarian no longer 'owns' the information since it is not contained within any physical institution; and it cannot therefore be 'managed' in the same physical sense. The information user, however, must still negotiate an information space, now across a digital network as much as before within the confines of a library, in order to achieve a successful resolution to the information transfer process.